On the Path to a World
of Tyranny?

Adolfo García Méndez

I

On the Path to a World of Tyranny?
© 2012 by Lemar Publishers
CreateSpace

ISBN-10: 1470133091
ISBN-13: 978-1470133092

Lemar Publishers
110 E Savannah, C-201
McAllen, Texas 78503
1-800-483-3223
956-631-7715
Fax: 956-687-4878
www.lemarpublishers.com
www.createspace.com

English translation of "Rumbo a la Tirania Mundial?" by Adolfo García Méndez, Lemar Publishers 2011, done by Paige Heisner (McAllen, Texas).
Technical revision: Leonardo J. Garcia
Portrait: Patricia Garcia Portillo
Typography: Leonardo J Garcia
Editor: LGM/Lemar Publishers

Printed in United States of America

Foreword

With a rarely observed capacity and observation analysis seen in the same person, with a deep desire to know and understand why things happen, Adolfo started more than 35 years ago to write journalistic articles in local and national newspapers in his country (Venezuela) about his thinking's , judgments and ideas about what was happening in and outside his country.

In this book *On the Path to a World of Tyranny?*, he discusses about the imminent dangers we are facing. Differences between a good and a bad government, between the Left and Right way of thinking are discussed, as well as suggestions to improve politically and economically any country, and by doing so, to make a better world.

Adolfo has a fabulous common sense, with a clear writing style rarely seen in a Latin-American author. I think it is very difficult not to agree with and understand his thinking's, to note the simplicity of his analysis and ground level examples on economical and political issues, which are the product of his long experience as a farming man. We will note in the book the logical consequences of political and economical policies that daily affect us. We will recognize the basic truths of this book, which fills in an empty space in the available literature dealing with Economic and Political topics, understandable to the common reading person. I consider this book to be a Political and Economical Bible ready available and with a basic and clear message for all who have the luck of reading it. Thank you brother for this book.

Dr. Leonardo Garcia Mendez
Pediatric Neurologist
Doctor in Medical Sciences
Retired Professor from Universidad del Zulia,
University of Missouri-Columbia and
The University of Texas Health Science Center at San Antonio

Appreciation

To my brother, Dr. Leonardo Garcia Mendez, for his foreword, and mainly because without his help, the publication of this book would not be possible.

Adolfo García Méndez.

PREAMBLE

Is material equality between people possible?

How far is humanity from being fully subjugated?

Have the communists disappeared along with the danger of world subjugation?

Who are those that are to blame for the great evils that we experience today?

Are the private means of production and service an obstacle for making a better world?

Why does the media have so much power, and in whose hands is that power?

What are the causes of the current economic crisis?

Why do oil prices increase so scandalously?

Who are the inappropriate governors?

Is the pluralism we know today beneficial?

Why are there still poor countries?

Where is the true exploitation of man by man going on today?

Are the Marxists excused from the damage they have caused others?

Are mandatory salary increases and price regulation beneficial?

We respond to all these and many other questions in this book.

And most importantly, we will realize that we should act soon, or ours could be the last generation to live in a free and independent country.

PART ONE

Motivations

Protagonists

The Circumstances That Compelled Us to Write this Book

A LITTLE HISTORY

Our uneasiness begins in the '60s, after having lived through the dictatorship of Pérez Jiménez in Venezuela and having observed the political and economic changes that came afterwards with the arrival of populist politicians and the enemies of free enterprise that had previously been exiled or in hiding.

In that time inflation was nonexistent, because the government did not get involved in questions of prices and salaries. But with the arrival of "democracy" and the enemies of private property, some things began to change for the worse. Seeing governors and political parties tolerating these irregularities caused us much concern. Why did they invade occupied lands that were producing? Why did they not respect the other? Why did they affect the economy of the country? In addition, there was no demand for land to be worked and to produce. It was the same political activists who organized the invasions and for this they recruited all types of people, including opportunists, who they brought to invade previously occupied and already planted lands. And the more livestock and milk they produced, the more they were branded – by the media– as owners of large estates, or landowners, words there had been unknown to us in that time.

Almost at the same time, the pre-existing association of producers began to give its support to one or the other politician from outside the realm of livestock farming. So too the children of the livestock farmers who had recently come out of university with their heads full of Marxists and anti-imperialist "teachings", gave their support to these outsiders. Among other things they were indoctrinated with the idea that developing countries were exploited by the transnational companies. This contributed to the resurgence of conflicts between producers and industrialists, which consisted in failing to provide milk to the industry until the prices increased by a certain amount. These conflicts, in our view,

3

did not have to exist. It was as if the tomato producers stopped selling to the sauce manufacturers, or as if the producers of fruits stopped selling them to the processors and packers of juices, seeking better prices when really these industries in all parts of the world are those that guarantee a better and greater market for the surplus. The livestock farmers entered into conflict with precisely those that, just a short time ago, had solved a great problem of the lack of a market for the surplus of milk. Additionally, independently of the fact that they could pay a better price, they got what was normal in a free market economy: that an association of producers – in this case milk producers– tried to obligate the industry to pay more than what they could or wanted to. In addition, these strikes were condemned to failure; the producers knew that they could only resist a few days without selling milk. But the government meddled with the situation, which perhaps was what the conflict's organizers had hoped for, and so the government began getting involved in questions of prices and salaries, and the people began to suffer, because each time the government pressured the industry, regulated prices of products, or decreed new increases of salaries, the prices increased as if by magic. These things concerned us, and for these reasons we humbly began to write.

MENTALLY FREE?

Why ask this question? Because it is very easy to find people who believe they posses truth, who tend to reject all that disagrees with what they previously accepted. Above all, having to do with topics in politics and economics, sciences which unfortunately are not exact like physics and mathematics and about which there has been much theoretical speculation. And closing the doors to our understanding is the same as converting our brain into an inalterable mass, without the capacity for dissent, like a disk that has been programmed by a computer. If we were this way we could only with great difficulty become aware of the reasoning of others, or be up to date with new knowledge or experiences that develop every day, above all in subjects as important for the wellbeing of everyone as political science and economics.

We are mentally free when we gain access to or are permitted to give space in our brains to all new ideas or thoughts without letting ourselves be influenced by the importance of the person who expresses it, nor by opinions of supposed "analysts." When we do this, our brain automatically takes in the most intelligent, the most logical: $2 + 2 = 4$; and rejects the illogical, the mistaken: $2 + 2 = 5$; this is what we very well could call our reasoning. Any person could be in possession of the truth, but could also be mistaken. What's important is not to close the doors to our understanding, because our brain needs ideas to be able to make comparisons with existing ideas, in order to then make our own conclusions.

Our brain needs to see and hear in order to judge. It is our judge. It is the brain with its extraordinary capacity for analysis, after adequate and prudent reflection that can make us see the difference between what is true and what is false, or between what we could consider good or bad.

Unfortunately in some countries with dictatorial regimes, the common man only has access to authorized interpretations, and in others, supposedly democratic, the enemies of the free press stealthily direct the principal means of information and opinion, such as editors, book distributors and book stores, so that the majority of people (many without knowing it) can only see, read or hear what they are permitted to.

TWO SYSTEMS: ENORMOUS DIFFERENCE

From the Bolshevik Revolution, when the Marxists took power by force in Russia, the world has been experiencing two very distinct government systems: the one previously addressed in Russia and many other countries, People of the Left, and the market and free enterprise system that prevails in the United States and also in other countries, People of the Right.

However, if we ignore the subjugation and other human rights violations of Marxist regimes, more that sufficient to cause us to distance ourselves from them, what, then, is the big economic difference between these two systems of government? Is it not the possession of the means of production and services? That with the first are in the hands of the party, and with the second are distributed among millions of owners? And what was, supposedly, the ultimate purpose of the Marxists? Was it not – supposedly—the wellbeing of the working class and of the whole world? And now, after one hundred years of governing Russia and other countries, in which countries and under which system are the workers better off? And in which countries and with which system are the citizens more free? Is it not in developed countries where free enterprise has always been respected? Is it not with the free market system? All this, it is important to point out, despite the grave and incalculable material and human damages that enemies of private property have done to these countries. It is a credit to the market and free enterprise system that free countries have progressed despite the damages done to them by the Marxists. It is sad that the sources of information and opinion never acknowledge these facts and never give them the importance that they really deserve.

And which countries prospered with the means of production and services in the hands of the party and without the help of the capitalists? And where are citizens more subjugated?

And if what the Marxists want is the wellbeing of the whole world, and especially of the working class, why then are they not on the side of those who create prosperity and wellbeing? Why, then, are they not with those who really respect their rights and permit them to enjoy liberty and wellbeing? Why, then, are they not with those who demonstrated that they are capable of bringing prosperity and wellbeing to all, especially to the workers, and have done so even while giving them complete liberty? Why, then, are they not with those in favor of free enterprise, or people of the right who want to collaborate with their country?

Another great difference between these two systems of government is that in free enterprise every individual can become important no matter how mediocre he may be. This is so because there are so many traits in people that each in his individuality is capable of developing. How many people make their fortune in a system of free enterprise without being very intelligent? How many could become an important person with a low level of intelligence in a system under the total control of the party? Unless it was in some athletic discipline, and they do not come to have the privileges that athletes have in systems of free enterprise.

Even the most insignificant people in the world can become important in a free country. They can even become important if they have the good fortune to win the lottery, which is somewhat restricted in a leftist regime. Well, what could they buy with such a fat prize if private property does not exist? Perhaps they could buy a business in order to have people to order around instead of having to always obey?

THE ADVERSARIES OF FREE ENTERPRISE

Without a doubt what is most reproachable about the enemies of free enterprises are the destructive and criminal practices of justifying any means in order to achieve their ends, a policy through which they still cause so much destruction. These practices probably are also responsible for the rejection of the communists throughout the world, for converting this ideology into a synonym for all evil, and they are only believed by those who ignore leftist procedures or in situations in which leftist's true beliefs are hidden. Perhaps also because of them the countries that became a part of the Soviet Union decided to stop calling themselves Communists in order to name themselves socialists.

But how could someone propose, and everyone else accept, the Marxist's policy of being able to use and justify all means – in which are included all evils- to achieve their ends? Perhaps it is because of these abominable practices that the great majority of the enemies of free enterprise do not identify themselves. And by not identifying themselves, they do more damage because they trick others easily; like those that launch themselves as candidates for important public positions; or those that direct or write in the media; or those that perpetrate multi-million-dollar cons or embezzlements. Because they neglect to identify themselves, many could think they are from the right; or the librettists and novelists whose work is to indoctrinate the minds of those that read their novels or see their movies or reports that capitalist society is a jungle filled with wicked, corrupt, and degenerate people capable of doing anything for money. And since now there are more producers of this type of movies and reportages (bought or founded by figureheads of the left) the damages they do are greater.

The enemies of private property also are experts in manipulation and for convenience are capable of trying to make us see green as black, or red as white, and for this

9

reason they call themselves different names according to the case. For example: by dividing Germany after the Second World War, the part that was annexed by the Marxists was called: Democratic German Republic, when everyone knew very well that it was democratic only in name. They also assigned names to the Marxist guerillas that expressed a desire for liberation although their goal was the complete opposite. Unfortunately some media outlets are faithful to this false nomenclature.

Now we observe how some countries where they have always respected private business are called socialist. So we would have two classes of socialists: Those that are in favor and those that are against free enterprise. In order to avoid misunderstanding, then, we will avoid using the terms socialist and socialism.

But then, what to call those that want the means of production and service to be in the hands of one party or one government? In the first place, we should clear up that many people have come to believe, perhaps because of manipulation and Marxist propaganda, that people that want the best for the poor are those of the left, and that the supporters of private enterprise, or of the right, are those wicked people without scruples, and it is for this reason that they consider themselves leftists, but they are not enemies of free enterprise. But who the hell has declared that because of the mere fact that people are from the right or the left will make them better or worse people than everyone else?

However, we cannot ignore that the Communists, just like the self-named socialists that integrated themselves into the Soviet Union, were or are enemies of free enterprise and are of the left, and that all the enemies of free enterprise are from the left. And that, of these, precisely because of these detestable practices of justifying any means to arrive at their ends, we can never know who lies and who tells the truth: not even when they lie and when they tell the truth and for this reason it is very difficult to know which leftists are enemies of private property, and which are not. And although, by their actions we could recognize them, we should make use of all of our intuitions in order to be able to identify them, because they can cause great damage.

For the same reason, we want to make clear that when we mention the left or leftists in these pages, we are referring exclusively to the enemies of private property. Likewise when we mention people of the right we are referring to the supporters of private property and free enterprise.

Another ruse or trick used by politicians from the left to get votes, is to propose new social benefits, but always with the money and the goods of others, generally with more taxes. This lacks virtue. There is no merit in giving or in sharing what belongs to another.

Paradoxically, the leftists prefer to live in capitalist countries because they enjoy the liberties that only this system can offer, although some of them do not appreciate it because they have had these benefits their whole lives, and because of this lack of understanding, they can even ignore that they are working in order to make it disappear.

Only by the nefarious practice of justifying any means to arrive at their ends and not knowing if they lie or tell the truth, it is a sufficient motive for not having confidence in them. The problem is being able to identify them.

THE WORLD CONTINUOUSLY CHANGES

We all realize how the world changes continually, how new inventions come on to the market and multiply our knowledge. So many, that at times, it is difficult for us to take it all in and become accustomed to all of them. Also, to the great majority of people, it was difficult to comprehend that the world was round when all the theories that existed at the time indicated that it was flat. It was not easy for people in that time to imagine that they were floating in space. We prefer to believe in simple things, and we dislike that which is complicated and difficult to understand. If we believe today in the Theory of Relativity it is not because we understand it but because we are told that it is true. In the end, it does not matter much to us if it is true or false. But suppose that this theory were very important to everyone, and that scientists' opinions were divided, that some tried to explain to us that time is relative and others told us that it is exact. Probably the great majority would be inclined to agree with the later, with those that assert that time is exact, because we measure it every day.

For the common man, it is easier to believe in the powers of a state with good intentions that wants to distribute equally to all, than to believe in the powers of free enterprise. In addition, the Marxists described their theories as "scientific," and perhaps because of this many people believed in them. Today we know how mistaken they were. For example: in reference to surplus value, we now know that the quantity of work that goes into merchandise is unequal in all places, depending on who directs the business and the form in which the product is produced. And surplus value can exist or not, depending on the efficiency and the mode of production.

It is true that the world changes continually. There are remedies that had been used for a long time to cure diseases that we do not use today because they are harmful or not effective. But let us suppose that the doctors of the past century, instead of prescribing the new medicine and putting into practice new discoveries, had held fast to the old treatments out of custom or stubbornness. Would medicine have advanced further? Without a doubt it would have stagnated, millions of people would have died and would have continued dying from diseases that today, fortunately, we can cure and prevent relatively easily.

In effect, what we knew yesterday is one thing, and what we know now is something very different. Let's suppose that today we need the services of a computer engineer. Would we look for one with the knowledge from three decades ago? Or suppose we needed to consult a specialist in some branch of medicine. Would we consult one with the knowledge from fifty years ago? How could we solve our problems in a successful way with people that are not up to date with the latest advances that are occurring in his field? And this fits for all specialties or professions, because, whatever the knowledge is, what we believed was best a few years ago, today we realize is no longer the most convenient. For this reason, what is normal, what is logical is that he who wants to exercise his profession successfully, whatever that profession may be should be up to date with new discoveries and experiences that are occurring in his field.

And if we know that doctors, engineers, mechanics, farmers, and other professionals are indispensable for the maintenance of the health, progress, and wellbeing of all, what could we say to those that dedicate themselves to political science and economics on which the future of all citizens depends and is at stake? Do we not all suffer the disgraces and calamities generated by lousy governors and inadequate political economies?

And if we know that Politics and Economics are not exact sciences like physics and mathematics, that there has been much speculation about its theories, and if we know of

13

the great responsibility that directing a country entails, and of how serious and delicate ignorance and the improvisation of the governors is, that we depend in large part on the experiences of other countries, and that it has to do with activities where wellbeing and the future of the whole world is at stake, how then at these heights of the 21st century in a country with a free enterprise system, can we still permit that mediocre people, without adequate preparation, and without being up to date with the most successful or disastrous political and economic experiences of the world come to hold such important positions? How is it possible that there are still not laws the prohibit people from occupying important public offices without having demonstrated honesty and loyalty to the system that they are going to represent or preside over?

If in order to assure the success of any mission in space the astronauts should have to pass hundreds of tests, shouldn't the candidates for important public positions have to submit themselves to tests of intelligence and all types of other tests, knowing that what is at stake is life itself and the wellbeing of all? Perhaps the prosperity of the country and the well being of the people is not the most important thing for everyone?

And if we know that all the inhabitants of a country, each one in his job, in the infinity of occupations that exist, from the most humble to the most prestigious, depends on the good administration of its governors, how then will a democrat that really wants the prosperity of his country and the wellbeing of his people permit people to occupy important public positions without first having demonstrated that they are ideal for holding these positions? How many countries are sunk in misery because of terrible governors? How, then, to understand that in the middle of the 21st century with such advanced technologies, there are no precise laws that stipulate that all people that seek to occupy important political offices should pass exams the prove their mental health, intelligence, capacity, and experience to administer and direct, honesty and responsibility, and above all, democrats and fervent defenders of private property and free enterprise? Who wants to have mediocre individuals in important public positions that in their heads internally sympathize with failed totalitarian regimes, and include in their practices lies, robbery, slander, blackmail, terrorism, and all evils that exist? How can we have confidence in and give a country over to people who are with both God and the devil?

CREATORS OF POVERTY

In order to know if something is harmful or beneficial, scientists base their studies in the law of averages: a ten percent difference above or below the norm is clearly conclusive. And if ten percent is enough, what could we say of those whose effect, in this case damaging and impoverishing, is one hundred percent? Without exception, all countries with a free market system and free enterprise, where enemies of private property have come to govern or form a part of the government, in some way became impoverished or backward, depending on the degree of radicalization and the timing of the intervention. On the other hand, all countries where the means of production were in the hands of the party, that open themselves to private investment, the free market, and free enterprise, prosper quickly. Examples abound. Why then do we permit governments or leftist candidates, if they all impoverish us, if they all create misery, if they all come to destroy, rob, and take our money for themselves? When and how could the enemies of private property progress without the help of those ingenious capitalists? Or when and how could they govern without submitting? If we add up the damages caused to many countries by the conflicts caused by the leftists, those who cause poverty, backwardness, scarcity of goods and food, unemployment, hunger and a lack of many necessities, plus the direct and intentional damages of guerillas and terrorists, we can affirm that almost all poverty that still exits in the world is caused directly or indirectly by the enemies of free enterprise. Poor people from those countries where the enemies of private property took power! How would the world be better today without these creators of poverty and conflict?

Explanatory note: To refer in this moment to the progress of China, which has continued to be a dictatorship, is to refer precisely to progress generated by free enterprise and private property in a country that permits it. Above all, they count on the unconditional support of all the information outlets and existing opinion in the country, and they do not have to suffer the serious damages that countries with free enterprise suffer through. This is the case in China. Perhaps dictatorships that are in favor of free enterprise always progress in this way, because they are able to impede a large part of the intentional damages done by enemies of private property, beside the support of the information outlets and the opinion media of the country, which all of the Marxist dictatorships have.

THE GREAT ENEMY

What has been the great sin of the North Americans? Why do the Marxists exert so much effort in causing bad things to happen to the United States? Could it be because they were the first to become independent, to cease being a colony, or because since then uninterruptedly they have the know how to live in democracy and then continued being the first and biggest in the world? Or could it be because they were the first to develop in most areas, despite the fact that the colonists arrived in North American lands more than one hundred years after they arrived in Latin countries? Or perhaps it is because North America holds within it millions of people of all races and creeds that seek a better life, or are fleeing tyranny? Or is it perhaps that they buy everything that we produce? Or because in the Second World War hundreds of thousands of North Americans gave their lives fighting against fascism, and they did not join the Germans as Italy, Japan, and Spain did? And the truth is that they were facing a great dilemma: to fight against the Nazis or against the Communists, to fight as allies of Stalin or as allies of Hitler. And what would have happened if the United States had joined against the Communists? And so why do the Marxists show such hate against the North Americans? Is it because they defend their freedom, including ours, and they have not let themselves be subjugated? Or because they try to defend themselves from terrorist criminals, that do so much damage to them and to everyone? Or is it perhaps because to them we owe a great petroleum industry, and the infinity of derivatives of petroleum, and even the automobile to use gasoline? Or perhaps because they are so stupid? Imagine that instead of sacrificing their country today or selling it in pieces to be able to buy petroleum at the exaggerated prices at which it is sold, they had bought lands before installing the costly and complex petroleum industries? Would Russia have given away the petroleum industry if it had been theirs? Or is it that we hate them because they taught us to treat and pay employees and workers well? Or perhaps it is because of the lack of favors "because they were not as generous as the

18

Russians, the Chinese, or the Arabs, to whom we own so many things?" Or is it perhaps because they invented the television, computers, cell phones and the Internet, and they "obligate" us to use them? Or is it because they invented light bulbs and air conditioning and thousands of devices that we use today, or for all of the advances and discoveries in medicine that save our lives every so often? Or is it because we have become accustomed to supermarkets and fast food, and large department stores? Or is it because they invented basketball and baseball, and they taught us to play, and they train our young men to take them to the Big Leagues? Or is it because we really hate them for being naive, for helping their enemies the Russians, Chinese, and others with great technology and investments?

And why do we so contemptuously call them (the United States of America) "imperialists?" Is it because they "damage" the countries where they arrive to invest? Or is it because by ending the Second World War, being the only ones that possessed the atomic bomb, they perfectly could have conquered the world, and however did not do it? Or is it because having been able to eliminate the ruthless and antidemocratic communist regime that from then on murdered millions of people and deprived hundreds of millions more of their liberty, and that still does so much damage to the world and to Americans, and however they did not do it? Or is it because after the Second World War, while the Russians annexed many European countries in order to enslave them in their system, the North Americans implemented the Marshall plan and provided their generosity and resources to help those countries that were devastated by the war, including its rivals? Or is it because they founded the United Nations with the goal of preventing other world wars, and provide economic help to the neediest nations, and to be, in addition, its principal economic contributor? And is it that they are so "imperialist" that they do not even take advantage to their atomic power to take democracy to other countries and instead they end the Second World War and then returned calmly to their homes? Or is it because of their ingenuity and good faith, or that they permitted many countries to fall into fierce communist dictatorships, including many that they themselves converted into great oil producers? Or is it because by wanting to defend other countries from the aggression of the guerillas or of the neighboring Marxist governments, they commit the serious error of sacrificing their people by facing them directly, instead of confronting decidedly those who arm them or train them, that really are the true aggressors and enemies?

United States of North America: "The Hen that Lays the Golden Eggs," the country where all races and cultures of the world live freely together. Refuge of all those that flee despotism and tyranny, where many would want to live, of which they want to eat, and from which almost all the world receives its benefits. And even so, they want to disarm and subject it, so that there remains no way out for these free men.

FALSE PLURARISM

Should democracies be "pluralist?" Is "pluralism" necessary for them to be called democracies? Is it beneficial? Who are those that really benefit from the pluralism that we know today? This is one of the great issues of some democracies, a problem from which many other problems derive.

We understand by political pluralism the right recognized in some democracies of the existence of all political currents, including those that are not democratic, like communism, fascism, or any other one, without worrying that their form of government has always been in the form of dictatorship. But, in what part of the world does a democracy exist with this type of pluralism? In the pluralism that we know today, they admit communists, but other parties that are no worse than communism, are not permitted.

The pluralism that we know today is based on the law of the funnel: meaning that it applies to the rivals, to the naïve, to the silly, meaning, it is okay for others, but not for me. You let me enter into your house and must attend to me in the best way, but in my house things are different, I don't even let you in, much less attend to you, nor do you have any rights. Really, the only ones that benefit from this strange pluralism are the Leftists in all their shades. Because, where the Marxists completely govern, no opportunity is given to the supporters of democracy and free enterprise, not in the press, not on the radio, not on television, not even in the sales of books and magazines, much less in publication. It is not even permitted to critique them.

The pluralism that we know today is an invention for those countries that practice silly democracy, naive democracy, that which sacrifices itself and lets itself be sacrificed, that which helps those who are not democrats. It is the law of the funnel: the wide is for you and the narrow is for me. Pluralism is only for free and democratic countries,

21

only for countries where the means of production and of service are in private hands. How can we understand why a democracy permits those who come precisely to end it to act freely? Does there exist in some place a democratic communism? And if we have never seen a communism or fascism that is democratic, and if we know that they are not democrats, why then do some democracies permit the communists to compete for power? How can they permit parties that only know how to lead by force and oppression, and whose end is to eliminate private enterprise and at the same time democracy and pluralism?

Democracy is one thing, and dictatorship is completely the opposite. It is like order and disorder, and one cannot have both at the same time. If you like order and you bring disorderly people into your house, you will never have order. If we like freedom, if we like democracy, how are we going to permit those who come precisely to put an end to freedom and democracy? Would it not be more intelligent to demand first that these parties show themselves capable of converting their dictatorships into democracies, and of permitting the supporters of private property and free enterprise?

The pluralism that we know today is the elegant form that the enemies of private property acquired so that they would be allowed to act freely. It is having the enemy in your bowels, and letting him act freely with his indoctrination in all fields of education, culture, religion, and in the areas of most influence and power, like the media. It is like letting your worst enemy into your house, and letting him pervert your wife and your children, and end up throwing you out or eliminating you and ending up with your house, your wife and your kids. It is like admitting a team that only came to obstruct, cause injury, and sew discord into a soccer championship, and the day that it wins a game, ends the championship by doing away with the other teams. Should this be permitted in a democracy? Should we let ourselves be manipulated like a stupid person with the pretext that democracies should be pluralist?

If we really value democracy, how are we going to permit others coming to annihilate it? Could those that support this pluralism be democrats? Do the communists give the same treatment to the supporters of democracy and free enterprise? Do they perhaps permit some minimal criticism in their closed and repressive dictatorships? It is as if someone has the right to occupy your house, and you have no right to occupy his house. But our imbecility goes beyond this: not only do we let them enter our house, but we also let them throw us out and they end up with our house. And some of the media go so far as to not only of let them enter, but also give them the best room, the best bed, and the best food. And to the supporters of free enterprise, perhaps they give the servants' quarters or a little area on the back patio. This is how things are. How can they give priority to the writings of people whose objective is precisely to do away with liberty and democracy? How can they permit political parties whose object is to do away with plurality?

There is not a single country where a true pluralism exists. Not in Venezuela, nor in Mexico, nor in Spain where they consent to communists but they do not permit supporters of a government like that of Francisco Franco. Nor in Chile where they want to condemn the Pinochet sympathizers despite the fact that all of these dictatorships gave more freedoms and were economically more successful than all of the communist and socialist dictatorships put together. However, they can swear, if anyone proposed in Spain that they admit a political party that wants to impose a government like that of Francisco Franco, the first that would protest would be the enemies of private property, because they are the only ones that benefit from this strange pluralism. And it is the pure reality, after they take power, or part of the power, they try by any means to take over all of the other powers, by tricking, robbing, and assassinating, and even simulating democracy. This is occurring in various countries.

EXCHANGING FREEDOM AND SUFFICIENCY FOR SUBJUGATION AND INEFFICIENCY

William James, North American philosopher and founder of pragmatism, affirmed: "The test of all truth resides simply in its efficiency."

In effect, if after knowing European countries with free market economies and free enterprise, or others like Canada, New Zealand, Japan, or the United States, all respectful of private property and capable of providing food, goods, and commodities of all types in abundance to all citizens and in complete freedom, it is difficult for us to comprehend that there are still people who are bent on destroying what has proved to be good, in order to exchange it for what has been a failure in all aspects. Perhaps, because as the refrain says: "No one knows a good thing until it is gone." Because if we reflect on the market and free enterprise system, never has anything been better: A system with such a degree of efficiency and creation of wellbeing, despite having to put up with constant aggression and other serious damages that are made by the leftists, among which are the current crisis that is dealt with later in this book. Even so, it is capable of producing and distributing wealth, goods, and services in such enormous quantities, not only to supply all of its citizens, but also its adversaries.

Not one country exists with a totalitarian leftist government that has not benefited from the direct or indirect help of free countries. They benefit from gigantic investments that create wealth, from their goods and foodstuffs. They benefit from their technology. And even from their purchases, with preferred trade status. Without going very far, Russia and other countries from the eastern bloc have received thousands of millions dollars in loans from the United States and other free countries. From the International Monetary Fund alone, of which the United States has been and is the principal provider of funds, in 1992 at the request of Washington, the institution hastened to loan Russia 1000 million dollars, 1500 more in 1993, and another 1500 in 1994. Later at the beginning of 1995 they conceded an additional loan of around 6000 million, and in March of 1996 it approved around 10,000 that was handed out over the course of the three following years. A total of 20,000 million dollars in just eight years. Do you know what twenty thousand millions are to Russia in just eight years? All this, in addition to other loans from other institutions, and technological help, and a qualified labor force.

Imagine that all of the wealth produced by North Americans and by other democracies of the free world, instead of being destined to help its ungrateful enemies, was used for the enjoyment of its own citizens. How many benefits, services and additional infrastructures would the North Americans would be receiving? However, the only thing they receive in exchange for this is damage. Why are the Marxists so ungrateful?

What is certain is that if it was not for their determination to impose on all of humanity a regime of slavery, and what's more a failed one, all of the countries on the Earth would be in much better social and economic conditions.

In effect, how can they want to exchange a system that has proved to be good and efficient for another that is failed and that the entire world detests for its falseness and for its inhumanity, in addition to being despotic and inefficient? Is it that the leftists, with good intentions, ignore what is happening? Is it that they do not realize because they are perpetually tricking one another? How can they want to impose a condemned system that lives in constant necessity, that is better off precisely because of the generosity of those that they want to eliminate? What do they gain by damaging those that help them? What satisfaction do they feel in trying to make people, including their own people, believe that what the entire world thinks is good is actually bad and that what everyone knows is bad is actually good? What satisfaction can they feel by trying to eliminate the system by which they live and eat? What merit would they gain by imposing a government that has been a failure in all aspects? What reasons could exist for trying to do away with this free and efficient system of government? Perhaps behind this great problem are the "teachings" that they still indoctrinate students with in many countries: the supposed goodness of Marxism and the apparent injustices of neoliberalism. It is a vicious cycle. Now instructed and believing they know the origin and the cure for all the evils, they turn themselves over to politics, or as journalists, "analysts," entertainers, or professors in order to continue instructing everyone else. Because they install themselves where the most damage can be done: like in political parties, in the media, in the universities, in the cinema and television industries, and even as clergymen of the different religions. Perhaps they do not realize that they are fooling themselves, and that the majority of the evils that the world suffers, excepting natural disasters, are the direct or indirect consequences of their actions.

WHO CAUSES THE CRISIS?

Why are the countries that are most affected by the global crisis those that need to buy a lot of petroleum and cannot recover the large amount of money they spend on it? And why does none of the petroleum exporting countries have financial problems?

And the financial crisis in the United States and in other countries exists because banks do not have the necessary funds to finance their normal operations. The money that the banks loan out is not being recovered the way it should. Mortgage loans are becoming delinquent. Credit cards as well. And a large amount of businesses are becoming bankrupt, among them the transportation companies and vehicle makers. And why do so many people not comply with their obligation to pay the banks? Because they also do not have the money and the principal cause was and continues to be the uncontrolled and completely abnormal increase in oil prices. Let us recall that in 1998 a barrel of crude cost between seven and eight dollars, and in less that ten years got as high as 150 dollars a barrel, meaning that the price of oil came to multiply itself by 20. And when countries do not produce sufficient oil to supply the consumption, it is their obligation to buy it. And to acquire it at abnormal and exorbitant prices has to damage them enormously. They are multimillion-dollar purchases that are carried out daily in the oil-producing countries. And this immense quantity of money that is spent is passed onto the citizens when they buy gas and its derivatives, which are many, or when they buy tickets for transportation, goods or food, which are also affected by the increase in the price of gas and of transport in general that are also incurred in addition to the costs of production. This also occurs with taxes because the government also increases its spending on oil and on all that they buy. But sometimes it is the government that pays the extra cost and subsidizes gas prices. And all these dollars that are added to the prices empty the consumers' pockets and are sent to petroleum exporting countries.

Unfortunately, gasoline and other oil products that come from petroleum is still indispensable. We cannot do without it. It is a necessary expense. The world economy would be held back. Air, land, sea, and river transport would be paralyzed. We should take into account that almost all of the motors that transport equipment and vehicles that are moved in throughout the world: ships, trucks, agricultural, industrial, and military machinery, were designed and fabricated for this type of gas and based on the prices that existed at that time. And all these great factories and industries that they constructed depended on these types of motors and vehicles. And this giant industrial structure cannot be changed overnight. There is not a single country that is in the condition to invest multimillion-dollar sums of money that would be needed to rapidly replace the existing structures. And additionally, most people are not in buoyant conditions so as to be able to substitute their vehicles for ones that consume very little gas.

There is no business or home in the United States that does not use at least one vehicle. And when countries do not produce the sufficient quantity of petroleum to keep up with consumption, they must buy it from elsewhere. And buying it at such abnormal and exorbitant prices must damage them enormously. And some more than others: above all those who are in a trade deficit that do not export enough to recuperate the millions of dollars that are imported. There is a lot of money that leaves the country and very little that is returned in exchange for domestic products.

And although many goods and services can decrease in prices because of the same scarcity of dollars and iron-willed competition, the businesses that produce them suffer the consequences of the increase in gas prices as well, working at a loss and even having to close, as has in effect occurred.

And because of all the money that is going to foreign countries, it becomes difficult for people to save, pay, and buy as they had before. And when they stop buying consumer goods, it also affects the stores that sell them and the businesses that make them. These businesses in turn, in order to even out their expenses and their earnings, will have to reduce their costs, amongst other things by firing employees and workers. And unemployment is the most nefarious part of any economic crisis. Because when the shopkeepers and manufacturers are affected because they don't sell as much as before, they are obligated to take measures to save their businesses, such as reducing the number of employees and workers. These workers are the most damaged because they can hardly buy essential things and it becomes more difficult for them to comply with their obligation to pay the banks, all of which affects the economy of the country enormously.

And so, in lesser or larger part, the people are affected by that lack of jobs and money, reducing their capacity to save and invest, and making it more difficult for them to comply with their obligations to pay their mortgage loans and credit cards, among other things. All of this has an enormous effect on the banks and the whole country in general.

And while the principal cause (high petroleum prices) of the crisis is not corrected, the measures that are put into practice are of very little value. Because in the cases where the governments inject money into the banks, it only serves as a mitigating factor, but it does not remedy the situation because the dollars will return to circulation and they will again be absorbed by the oil exporters. In addition, the money for such aid would be obtained through the sales of treasury bonds, however when it comes time to pay them, it would come out of the taxes that the citizens have to pay. Meanwhile, the money that goes out of the country and that ordinarily should be returned to buy the things that are internally produced, many times takes a long time to return because the oil-producing countries invest them or deposit them in other countries. And when the money is finally returned the damage is already done, because the money is probably tied up in treasury bonds, which increase the debt of the country. Or it is tied up in buying businesses, above all media outlets that the oil producing countries will use to eventually take over everything.

But the high oil prices are not the only thing to damage the United States and other countries. The damage is also done in other ways. For example: it is the ruling regime in Venezuela who stockpiles money, and authorizes and pays for all imports. This regime surreptitiously went about denying purchases from the United States, unless the products could not be acquired in other places. And even still, they intentionally did not pay many companies for the purchases they made. To General Motors alone, they owe two thousand million dollars. Logically, as strong as the economy of a country may be, these intentional damages seriously affect the businesses and make the crisis worse. In contrast to their comrades, the Chinese and the Russians, they have given thousands of millions of dollars, in exchange for supposed satellites and armaments, with which they buy businesses all over the world, or treasury bonds in the United States, or in other countries to put those countries even more in debt.

Disloyal competition also damages the United States. For many businesses that are affected by the rise in gas prices and the costs of production, it is more difficult to compete with those from outside, where gas and labor are much more economical. In the same way it is difficult for international air transport companies to compete with those that are supplied with more economical gas because their "proprietors" are from oil producing countries.

Other countries are also affected by the crisis, because nations like the United States that could invest, visit as tourists, and buy many things from them, now cannot do it like they could before, precisely because they are in the middle of a crisis.

WHY HAVE OIL PRICES INCREASED SO MUCH?

Monopolies are perverse. Their goal is to monopolize and control production in order to impose prices and for this reason they are prohibited in many counties, although, not by chance, they are only prohibited in countries with a free market and free enterprise system. Why would this be? However, internationally, the largest and most damaging economic monopoly in the world has been created, OPEC, and the media does not denounce it, as if it were the most normal thing in the world. And why do they not denounce it? Because unfortunately, the larger part of the media, just as many member countries of OPEC in complicity with Russia, are in the hands of the left and they use their profits to continue stockpiling media outlets, and above all stockpiling world economic power. And how will the media denounce the fact that the crisis is caused by exaggerated prices of crude oil, if the media is also responsible for making the prices go up? (Just as they also do not inform us that the prices will go down for some reason, as in effect has occurred.) For example: in the tragedy of New Orleans some refineries were ruined. It would have been a good moment to announce that because of the tragedy a large quantity of oil would be unable to be processed and for this reason the prices would decrease. But the media did the opposite, and announced that because of the tragedy, the petroleum prices would go up and they made them go up.

There is no single fundamental motive for bringing up the oil prices. There is no shortage of oil. There is more than sufficient oil for world demand. The most palpable test is that each time that oil prices decrease, this monopoly announces a decrease in production in order to increase prices. This, along with alarmist information about supposed incidents in producing countries, and the declarations of apparent "analysts" that are in the media, push prices up. But the harsh reality is the they continue selling all the petroleum that they are asked for, they just stop selling the inevitable decreases in consumption that are precisely due or related to the high prices. The test of this is that according to data from the U.S. Energy Information Administration, the consumption of petroleum in the last few years has been greater than production. This seems unlikely, because how is it possible to consume more than what is produced? In other words the supposed reductions are only to manipulate and blackmail the buyers, who, without a doubt, have let themselves be extorted with the prices. Because, just as the exporters of crude oil and their intermediaries come to an agreement to increase prices, the consumers must do the same in order to not be blackmailed, and not pay more than what they had agreed upon previously. Because, just as many countries need to buy petroleum, the producing countries also need to sell it. And it is necessary to lower crude oil prices to exit this perverse crisis and avoid prolonging it. If we continue permitting this monopoly to continue imposing crude oil prices, it will be very difficult to get out of the crisis. And the worldwide disaster caused by the left could be irreversible.

No monopoly is justifiable, and if they cannot be prohibited at a world level, their dominance could increase. Producers of other minerals, or foodstuffs, or chemical products, or any other product could follow suit.

Let us suppose that the principal wheat and milk producing countries create a monopoly in order to increase the prices to many times the actual value of their products, what price would we have to pay for wheat flour, bread, cheese, and all the derivatives of these essential staple foods? If this were to happen, would the UN continue to allow it to happen as well? And would the media also let it happen? Do they not have the obligation to denounce the monopolies? Will they turn a blind eye while people the world over bear the burden of all types of hardships? Because although it doesn't seem that way, the monopoly created to increase the price of crude oil is much more damaging that the hypothetical one to increase the prices of wheat and milk because these foods can still be substituted with other products. In contrast, gas derived from petroleum is more difficult to substitute in an immediate form for the reasons already exposed in the previous article.

What is certain is that this monopoly was created to increase crude oil prices – in complicity with Russia and the leftist media – and has caused a crisis in many countries that need to buy gas. And if the UN does not immediately intervene in order to break this monopoly and make the crude oil prices return to normal, the world disaster could be irreparable.

But the most absurd thing is that there is few oil exporting countries where people really benefit from the high prices, because the money is not used to increase the quality of life of the population. Clearly we see that they are not interested in the wellbeing of the people. So much so that in Venezuela, despite the crude oil prices that multiplied themselves by twenty, the employees and petroleum workers of the State make less money today than they earned ten years ago, and the highways of the country are in a deplorable condition because none of this money is spent on the maintenance of infrastructure.

UNSUITABLE GOVERNORS: WHO ARE THEY?

The greatest injustice that unfortunately countries with a free market still experience is that people that in their heart of hearts do not support the free market system come to hold important government positions. This people are inwardly not in agreement that the means of production should be in private hands. These are people that in their heads, internally, are enemies of the free enterprise system and are unsuitable to govern a country with a system in which they do not believe. The unsuitable governors always leave the country in worse condition than when they took office. Because when these people hold such positions, their interest is not in helping the system of free enterprise, but rather in taking advantage of their position in order to benefit their beliefs. And they betray the country that they promised to help, when all the citizens had confidence in them to protect it.

We all know that in free countries the economy rests on millions of proprietors. That the whole economic complex that countries like the United States, Mexico, and Canada are content with rests on and supports millions of enthusiastic citizens. And when in these countries confidence in the government is lost or is not sufficient, fears increase, the mood falls, enthusiasm is lost, and the great motor that moves the economy decelerates. For these countries, unfortunately unprotected from their worst enemies, the unsuitable governors are like wolves disguised in sheep's clothing, because all people had confidence in them and voted for them, yet they betray their country. A good example of this type of governor is Obama, who promised to do everything possible so that the United States did not depend on foreign oil. And what has he done with respect to the subject? Has it not been completely the opposite? Do the measures that he took to prevent further accidents in the Gulf of Mexico help the United States? We will mention some:

suspending the exploration along the coasts of Alaska, cancelling the pending concession in the Gulf and the proposed concession on the coast of Virginia, maintaining the current moratorium and suspending the signing of permission for new drilling in deep waters, and suspending the activity of 33 exploratory wells that at the time were being drilled in the Gulf? How much petroleum have they continued importing because all those wells in construction and in progress now do not produce? And how many people are now without work during this crisis? Let us recall that for the Marxists "the ends justify the means." For this reason they pretend to want to help their country and the most needy, while really impoverishing them and subjugating them. They trick people, and for this reason they invent new benefits and expenses from more debts and more taxes, all the while knowing that they are causing damage and giving rise to unemployment. And they disarm the United States. They deny it defense projects, while externally they are complacent with all dictatorial leftist regimes. And they help them such regimes economically. These people take advantage of their comrades – the unsuitable governors – in order to make themselves stronger militarily, economically, and politically, and to take power in more countries.

The worst that can happen in free countries is to be governed by unsuitable governors, because they pretend to help, while really they cause damage in all aspects. And they discourage the millions of proprietors on which all the economy rests and is supported. Meanwhile, the media (the principal weapons that they use to induce people to elect them) will continue trying to make people believe that what they are doing is good.

Unfortunately, while in the totalitarian leftist countries all the media are property of the system, and all the news and opinions are controlled and authorized by its dictators, in free countries they can also be bought, and new ones can be established, and or they can all be taken over. This is happening. Many still do not notice this very serious problem. And they even let themselves be manipulated by the media. And if things continue as they are, very soon we will all be subjugated, as we explain later in the book when we talk about the powerful media.

AND WHO LIKES TO LIVE SUBJECTED?

Let us suppose that they invent a new system of government in which its creators believe blindly. This system will supposedly bring more comfort and wellbeing than all other previously known systems and it has many sympathizers. Do you think that because its creators and sympathizers think that it is the best system of government, they have the right to trick others, and to eliminate their opposition, and obligate the whole world to accept the system for better or worse? And if we know that nobody has a reason to cause harm to his fellow men, and less for denying to accept something that he wants to impose, how, then, do Leftists expect to obligate the whole world to accept a system known and characterized by the despotic, by lies, by thieves and criminals, and on top of all that, one which has failed? Unfortunately it is happening.

Today let us imagine that the workers are already submitted and forcibly divided into two very different classes: the governing class, which possesses all the privileges, and to which without a doubt, everyone will want to belong. And the submitted class, which should and has to obey, and to which no one will want to belong. Now my friends of the left, although today you think that you could be in the governing class, imagine that you are included in the submitted class. Do you know that it means to be condemned for life to being workers and employees of the sole proprietors, and without any sort of right to complain? Do you know what it means to not be able to do anything without the consent of the masters? Do you know what it means to live perpetually submitted? That whiles the masters make and unmake (in the name of the people), you have no value at all.

But what gives them that right? Why do they want to obligate people to live in a system that they do not like? Who could like having to obey their whole life? Who could like being a slave forever? Why do they want to impose on the whole world a system of slaves simply because they have that desire, so robbing them of their votes, or tricking the whole world, or eliminating those that oppose them? Why, with what right, why do they want to obligate everyone to live in a system that they do not like? What supreme authority authorizes them to take over a country, its people, and its goods? Do they know what it is to live eternally submitted? Why so much hypocrisy: days of parties, offerings, and commemorations to our liberators, if they are not capable of honoring them by defending what cost them so much blood, lives, and time? What would our liberators do if they lived with us today?

Are they conscious of what it means to betray their country and their brothers in order to submit them to a global foreign command, and without knowing how they are going to be treated? Are they so naïve as to not realize that they are being used so that they can latter be thrown out with the trash? What other motive could there be for damaging these economies knowing that with them there is progress and the working class is better off? What other motive could there be for continuing to damage businesses knowing that they create wealth and wellbeing for the whole world, and above all for the working class? What other motive could there be for continuing to damage, trick, and rob precisely those that want to transform their backward countries? Is it understandable that because of this stubbornness, thousands of people have to flee their country and millions go through hunger and necessity? How can they want to submit their countrymen to a foreign political and economic power?

Let us imagine that 150 years ago they had installed globally the system that the left wants, with all the media in the hands of a small group. Would the enormous quantity of goods and services and the thousands of modern technological advances that today we fortunately use and enjoy exist? What was the motive for Russia and China to open their doors to the businessmen of free countries, if not precisely to try to achieve the prosperity that their system of slaves could not acquire? How can they want to eliminate a system that has proved in many countries to be capable of bringing wellbeing to all, including to the very leftists that also live in it and enjoy it along with their families?

If Marxism was a regular system of government, why would it need to wait so that the system that "does not work" (that of the free market and free enterprise) develops the means of production and service in order to later takes them over? Why would they need to trick people? Is it because of all this that the great majority of the enemies of free enterprise do not identify themselves? Would the people vote for them if they knew? Would people have voted for Obama if he had identified himself as an enemy of free enterprise? Why do the very Marxists themselves not like to live in the countries where the means of production are in their hands? How many families would leave those countries if they were permitted to? They can be sure that if the Marxists do subject us all, we would all want to leave if we could, even many leftists themselves. Is it for this reason that they don't want to give us even a little free space where we could go to live?

ARE THE MARXISTS GIFTED IN EVIL?

All beliefs and doctrines, be they political or religious, have their followers or supporters. And everyone thinks that his or her belief is better. For the believers in Mohammed and the Koran, there is nothing that comes close to Islam. For a true democrat, democracy is the best system in the world. The Nazis think that the world would be better under National Socialism. For a practicing Catholic, the Catholic Church is the true religion. It would be difficult to convince a Marxist fanatic that there is something better. As the popular refrain says: "Each head is a world" or "To each his own". But the fact that some love their religion or political beliefs does not give them a right to kill or cause damage to others in some way because they do not share their beliefs? Can these beliefs cause us to dispose of life, liberty, and the money of others with impunity, to supposedly facilitate, promote, or finance the doctrine in which we believe? The tragedy that the Jews, victims of the political fanaticism of the Nazis, fierce believers in National Socialism, experienced in the Second World War is not far off. However, the whole world knew of these crimes and those responsible for this genocide, in addition to winning universal condemnation, were searched for, persecuted, arrested, and punished with the death penalty or life in prison. There was no person in the world that would ask for clemency for these criminals. Much less because they were made in the name of a political party in which they believed and professed as the best on Earth.

Today, at the beginning of the 21st century, we are perplexed by incalculable technological and scientific marvels. However, in the social, political, and moral aspects, without a doubt we have regressed. The crimes that we see today in the name of religious creeds or political ideologies are more abominable than those that the Nazis perpetrated. They are above all cowardly, because they are committed in free democratic societies where everyone can exercise the right to have an opinion and to spread his or her ideas in a civilized and peaceful manner. These crimes are executed in the most vile, treacherous, and repugnant manner that exists: buildings filled with innocent people are blown up to sew fear and terror. Planes filled with passengers are made to explode mid-flight. Age, sex, and race do not matter, and it doesn't matter if there are women, children, or elderly people. Whole towns are massacred by fanatical Marxist guerillas. Policemen, humble people in small towns that try to earn their living in this work just like everyone else, are assassinated. They explode oil pipelines and sources of clean water causing serious ecological damages and irreversible environmental catastrophes. And they finance themselves with something as deplorable as drug trafficking and the kidnapping of people who they murder if they do not comply with their demands. Truly, it seems like a curse has fallen on the Earth. It is not a coincidence that terrorism and guerrillas act only in countries with a free market and free enterprise system. Marxist fanaticism has caused more deaths that the last two world wars. It is incredible that these multiple and cowardly murders are still committed. But what is most alarming and worrying is the indifference of the media that the world become conscious of the magnitude of the evil and the crimes they commit. So it seems that the Nazis could very well use gas chambers again to continue killing innocent people, and go unnoticed. As if international organizations and the media did not have the professional and moral responsibility of denouncing and getting these criminals punished with the severity they deserve. (Above all those who plan, arm, and train those who carry it out.) It is alarming how some governments and international organizations are indifferent to these genocides. It is perplexing, because some governments even give protection to these criminals. And they even go so far as to justify them, interview them, and even take them to the big screen or the small screen as protagonists.

Would the Marxists agree with these practices if they were the victims, if they were the kidnapped, tortured, and massacred, and if some governments trained, armed, and protected their killers? Would they justify the terrorist acts because they were done in the name of a political ideology? Would they pardon all of the crimes committed because they were supposedly for a good cause? Would they elect them to preside over a country, or to serve as senators or representatives, and would they treat them as heroes?

He who murders in cold blood in order to supposedly benefit his beliefs deserves more severe punishments than he who does so for other reasons. What believers do not think that their doctrine or religion is the best and the true one? And does that give them the right to rob, kidnap, and murder others? No one possesses the right to commit crimes, much less does a country or leader possess the right to protect, tolerate, or treat give special privileges to those who commit the vilest murders in the name of a religion or political belief. Bolivar said it well: Violence is the weapon of those that do not have reason. The violence can only be justified before totalitarian regimes, when people in the opposition are not permitted the spread of ideas.

THE TRUE CRIMINALS

If a madman kills people, the right thing to do is imprison him so that he doesn't murder anyone else. But if someone hides him, or makes the search for him more difficult, or knows where he is hidden and does not say so, while he continues murdering people, who, then, is the real murderer? And what do we say about those who arm, train, and brainwash these people, who put them in a car filled with dynamite, or place a bomb on their body or send them to explode next to hundreds of innocent people? Or of the media that instead of condemning and accusing those who hide them, arm them, and train them, criticize the governments or leaders that confront them in some way? How can they reproach the governments that try to protect their countries and their citizens from these massacres and multiple murders? It is like blaming the police for combating criminals. They want to convey to the good people that the murderers should be left alone, that we should stop looking for them, or even gratify them in some way so that they stop killing, or else they will continue to threaten and kill. The same media prepares the blackmail of the devil and spreads it repeatedly so that the whole world accepts it. And they manipulate the masses in such a way that many end up accepting the blackmail and welcoming the withdrawal of the forces that defend us from evil. And sometimes people do not even realize the manipulation that they are the objects of.

These individuals that in some way justify these criminals are the true murderers, because they go so far as to interview them and transmit their messages and recordings, and even bring them to the big screen or the small screen to convert them into heroes. They do what the terrorists want. They do precisely what they should not. And it is not that they do it without realizing, because the consequences of this conduct have been known for some time and reviewed by psychologists and psychiatrists. For example: some years ago we could observe many fans in the stands that threw themselves to the ground level in order to become "streakers"

45

and come out on television. And they even got applause from the public. They wanted to be seen as daring individuals. They wanted to feel important. This brought, as a consequence, the proliferation of the reckless and daring. And each time there were more people who threw themselves onto the field. Some team owners and authorities even came to an agreement so that they were ignored and at the same time punished for interrupting the spectacle. Today the cases are very isolated and it is clear that all now condemn them. The media should behave similarly, and with very good reason, if they really want to eradicate terrorism. In the first place they should condemn these acts for how monstrous they are. In the second place, they should never give notoriety to the protagonists. Never ever interview them, or publish their messages, and much less justify in some way their criminal acts, because this is precisely what they want. What the media and the journalists should do more of is investigative work and collaborations until these criminals are detained and punished. Above all those who finance, arm, train, and protect, that are the real killers. But on top of all this, some media outlets blame the governments of the countries that confront them. So we observe the unjust criticism that was made toward the United States because they wanted to stop the rise of terrorists after the cowardly and monstrous criminal act at the Twin Towers, where thousands of people of different nationalities died. Certainly, on September 11, 1973 the Marxist regime was overthrown in Chile. Could it be a coincidence that the terrorist act also occurred on an 11th of September? Such is the manipulation of information with these biased analysts that we never heard said that those to blame for the deaths in Iraq are those who arm, train, and convert those unfortunate people, into explosives and criminal human bombs, just as those that harbor them are also responsible. They even go so far as to make movies or documentaries where the terrorists are the protagonists. This can only mean that all of them just like those that financed and protected them, form a part of the same conspiracy.

AND EVEN SO, IT PROGRESSES

Without a doubt, the actions of the enemies of free enterprise, with their Machiavellian practices, has been terrifyingly damaging for all of humanity. This includes, in addition to the monstrous terrorist acts, scandalous looting of the money of the people in many countries. However, the free market system is so effective that despite the serious damages that are intentionally done to it, even so, it progresses. But, today, would the world not be a thousand times better without these continuous and severe damages? China is a great example of how a country can prosper when they permit private property and let the free market and free enterprise system function in an environment of peace, without the inconveniences and the damages that capitalist countries must support on the part of the leftists.

Let's imagine that at the same time that Russia was subjected to Marxist totalitarism, the rest of the world had been as well. What would have happened? Would we not have been able to reach the magnificent advances that we have in science and technology today? Would we not still be anchored to the technology of the 19th century? And not even dreaming of looking for financial aid and technology from the West, as on repeated occasions the leftists have, above all in recent years? Without a doubt, we would all be in the same backward state. Or perhaps worse, because, by eliminating in that time the enemies of the proletariat (the machines), we would still be working rudimentarily. And with what crystal ball would we have been able to witness the surprising technologies and the consequent wellbeing that, thanks to them, today we can enjoy, and the illnesses that today we can prevent and cure, and the marvelous satellite communications, and the infinity of products and entertainment that make life today easier and more pleasant? And what would have happened if Russia and other countries of Europe had not been subjugated by the Marxists, taking into account the entrepreneurial spirit of these Europeans, and that the majority of the imprisoned and executed people

47

in those countries were among the most educated and intelligent? Would the world today not be more developed and advanced in all aspects? How would the world be today if the leftists, instead of using all means – in which all evils are including – to derail peace, progress, and development in capitalist countries, they had collaborated with them the same way they do today in China? And for what reason does those who always believed in democracy and in private property, never organize to defend themselves? This is without a doubt the principal failure that democracies still have, that very few defend themselves from those who do them so much damage. Perhaps because in free countries the first preoccupation of the people is bettering their conditions of life and of their family, and trying to overcome those challenges every day, and there is no more time left for politics unless they are affecting him, which is the case today. Or because they see private property as it really is: something natural that has always existed. Even the very animals defend their territories instinctively.

And what was so bad about it that caused the supporters of private property to freely win so many enemies? Perhaps the private business that today operates there damages China?

Perhaps in the background of the great problem is that not all people are pleased by the progress of others. It was enough for them to read something that said that it is unjust that some have and others do not, to dedicate their lives to criticizing and causing problems for others.

SECOND PART

In this part we analyze a series of facts, affirmations, myths, and fallacies that for much time have been wielded and put into practice by Marxists against the system of free enterprise and private property, and with which they have been able to recruit and confuse many people.

IS MATERIAL EQUALITY POSSIBLE?

Our intention is not to elaborate on the way in which some things occurred in the evolution of man. We only want to clarify that inequalities form a part of the human condition.

Since men have inhabited the earth, differences have existed between them, just as there are differences between animals. It will be difficult to find two people with the same patience, will, intelligence, memory, bravery, or optimism. It will be difficult to find two people equal in even one of the infinity of aptitudes, vices or virtues that some possess and that others do not have. These great differences were those that made it possible for many of our ancestors to evolve slowly, until they became man as he is today. And it is perhaps also due to those great differences that many stayed behind and still remaining savage. But among those who evolved there were also differences; they exist even today, and they will exist even among clones.

Probably in that time the first man, on seeing a cave, thought that he could be more protected from the sun and the rain there, and decided to live there with his family, thus producing the first material inequality between them: those that had a home and those that did not. And although this ancestor had little merit, he still thought and acted, and this made him different. And there would be another who took a heavy piece of wood by one of its extremities, would think that it could defend him better, or do more damage to his rival. This human also set a precedent: he was perhaps the first armed man that existed, and could well have become the chief of his tribe. And there would be another that by finding a sharp stone thought that he could use it as a tool to cut, whittle or improve his combat weapon. And others would emerge with new ideas that they would put into practice and that would give them other advantages for defending themselves, or for feeding themselves, or for making their lives safer and more pleasant, and that without a doubt made them stick out and seem different from the rest. And the day would arrive in which someone collected nuts, coconuts or other dry long-lasting fruits from the time of abundance and kept them for the days when food was scarce, which without a doubt put him in an advantageous situation compared with others. And there would be another who was more curious who observed the germination of seeds of known edible fruits and had the idea and the will to collect them and sew them close to his home to observe them and care for them. And the first farmer probably emerged in this very way. And there would be others that by seeing those first results, also began to collect and sow grain and entered into the group of the hard working, willful and cautious.

And it is probable that some made fun of those first "stupid" humans who at times did not eat because of trying to stock up on fruit or plant grain. And they never planned; they preferred to live as they always had; when there was food to eat, they ate, and when there was not, they endured it or they died.

Now here we can observe some differences between those first primitive men: those that worked and those that did not, those that saved and those that did not, those that planted, cared for, and harvested and those that did not do it, those that were better fed and those that were badly nourished. Two classes of beings that through time became very different: those that evolved and those that lagged behind. But, however, all of them lived in freedom and did what they wanted. And while some remained savage, some left that category.

Now let us imagine living in those primitive times with ideas of equality and class differences among humans and that there already existed a chief to which everyone obeyed and that in the name of equality and the most needy, he ordered all the grain that had been put away by those first farmers to be confiscated, in order to be distributed amongst those who had nothing. Perhaps the first consequence of obligating them to turn over what they had planted, cared for, harvested, and kept with such care, would have been the loss of independence and freedom, as much individual as of the group. Surely those pioneers of agriculture would not have planted or kept grain tucked away, at least voluntarily. This would have had the serious consequence of reverting to a savage state. And if they were obligated to sew and harvest, then they would have established, as so many other times in the history of man, two very different and unequal classes: those that mandated and those that obeyed, the masters and the slaves.

Now let us move to the time when the communist movement was initiated and the Manifesto was published for the first time. And let's suppose that they had had sufficient political support to install communism globally. What would have happened? Let us start with one of the "injustices" that the Marxists always criticized about private enterprise. According to these theorists, the privileged class, in its desire for profit, devised the idea of "exploiting" or firing the workers, and for this reasons invented machines which still make it possible in factories or in private agricultural farms to increase production with fewer workers, and without the necessity of increasing them. Without a doubt, one of the first decisions of the communists would have been to eliminate these enemies of the proletariat, to prohibit their invention and construction. This would mean that we would be condemned to systems of productions that existed in that time. It would mean condemning us to stagnation and to continuing to live almost primitively. It would mean subjecting all of us from that moment on. And when people lose their freedom by being obligated to live in a regime that they do not want to, when people lose freedom because of the imposition of a regime that monopolizes information, opinion, and ideas, that tricks and distorts the facts, that hoards production and the trade of goods, then the class difference is immensely greater, and infinitely larger the inequality between those that lose liberty and those that take it away.

It is very easy to make a group of people equal by taking away from those that have and distributing it among those who do not have, in such a way that all are materially equal. But, how many days could it remain that way? They could even make them all naked, in such a way that they did not possess anything. But even so, in just a few hours, if they were allowed to, some would look for a way to be more sheltered or more comfortable, and could make a bed or a blanket. And now this lone act of possessing a bed or a blanked, while the others lack everything, would make them immensely rich and unequal in comparison to the others.

Only partially and by force could we arrive at material equality between people. Only partially and by obligation could they make a group of people materially wealthy. History is filled with movements or revolutions in the name of equality, but it has not been possible to achieve. The very act of wanting to impose it creates inequality. There will always be a greater inequality between those that impose it and those that submit to it. And the more they try to impose it, the greater the inequality will be. The best example: the dictatorial Marxist regimes. But why seek equality in slavery and poverty instead of trying to obtain it in prosperity and freedom? Is it not preferable to try to obtain less material inequality between the people without losing freedom? One way is trying to stimulate those who lag behind, if what you want is to improve and overcome, and another is giving protection when it is necessary. The stimulus to overcome is important, but also acts in an unequal way. In a market and free enterprise system, as time goes by, some of the poor will overtake the richest, others will become equal, others will worsen in condition and others will fail completely, but at time of comparison, there will always exist inequalities, because it is logical and natural. Without liberty, we could very well blame the inequality in which we live on those that have us submitted. But they should never blame others for the material inequality in which they exist if they had the same liberties and opportunities to do what they wanted to. In liberty, there will always be people who want to rise up, to improve, to be more than others, to seek more comfort, and to become important. But a person, or a hard-working people that has risen above, cannot be to blame for the others that are in unequal or worse economic conditions.

DO THOSE WITH MORE MONEY WORK LESS?

The Marxists note that the capitalists can live without working. But as the wise refrain says so well: "There's a big gap between what is said and what is done." Perhaps the bosses that work more hours in a day than their employees and workers are rare? Or perhaps administrators of state business work more than the owners of private businesses in the countries with a free enterprise system?

How many times do we hear owners criticized for their frugal way of life, despite having large properties? They live poor and die rich. This way of life so frequently among producers of the livestock raising region of my birth, Perija, was what inspired a great personality from the same region, Remigio Rincon, the popular "Perico," one of his celebrated sayings: "The perijaneros are like yuca (tapioca), they produce only after they are buried". This means that while living, very few realized the fortunes they possessed, and that only after being dead and buried was the great capital they possessed made known.

Today the political and personal insecurity that exists in Venezuela, the kidnappings and murders, the disrespect for private property, the invasions of fields and terrain and its possible confiscation at any moment, caused not only that the producers of the rural areas work now with less enthusiasm and take things more cautiously, but also that they learned to enjoy more what they have.

The very same Remigio Rincon incarnated the completely opposite way of life from that of the producers of the region. He was a simple seller of vehicles, but very esteemed because of this simple way of life: always joyful, well-dressed, with a good car, and there was not a party or a dance in the towns in the region that could not count on the pleasure of the presence of the popular "Perico," always well accompanied. These cases are not rare nor are the

55

exceptional, and one sees or hears anecdotes about people like this in all towns and cities. What we want to clarify is this: that the rich do not always live better than the poor, nor do the poor always live worse than the rich. And this, considering it exclusively from the material perspective, because if we analyze it from the spiritual point of view, or the internal happiness of a person is precisely what maters most, without a doubt we would find the happiest people in barrios and the poorest places of the city, rather than in the most well-to-do sectors of society.

THE MYTH OF THE DISTRIBUTION OF WEALTH

Much has been speculated about the supposed "Distribution of Wealth" as a formula for eliminating poverty, as the remedy for elevating the standard of living for those who have little or nothing. And we hear about it every so often from politicians and religious people, and their intermediary "analysts" and journalists.

This is one of the great fallacies of recent times. Naturally some goods can be distributed in a given moment among the most needy, but this will never bring the poor to a long-lasting wellbeing. Probably, far from contributing to improving their quality of live, what it does is impoverish them even more. The great error and confusion stems from facts being perceived the reverse of how they should be perceived. Specifically, they see wealth as if it has always existed, which is false, and as if someone had taken advantage of it and had left nothing for others.

If we arrive in some unknown region of the world and we encounter all the inhabitants of that region living in a primitive way, plagued by disease, malnourished and in extreme poverty, we couldn't blame anyone, or say that they have their problems because they did not distribute wealth. In effect, who would we blame if everyone lived in a state of poverty? But if at the moment of arriving in that region we encountered some living better than others and they got the idea in their heads of constructing and having better houses, that they planed and ate better than the rest, then probably yes, we would criticize them for the inequality in which they live. It is here when we reason and act backwards; instead of recognizing the merit of those who put forth effort and progressed, and inspired those who were still living in the primitive way to overcome their surroundings as well, we think, on the contrary, of taking from those who put forth the effort in order to give to those who did not do anything. We think of taking from those who through much work and

57

sacrifice progressed, to give to those who made no effort. This, of course, discourages those who did put forth that effort, and accustoms those who did not do anything to getting things they do not deserve.

Currently it is very rare for a poor person to be criticized for his apathy or for his lack of spirit to overcome obstacles. Neither do we criticize a middle class person that has had a business stagnate for many years with the same personnel, with the same furniture, and that contributes very little to the progress of his country. But in contrast, we criticize those who made their businesses grow: the ambitious, those that prospered, those that saved and made the effort, those that had good ideas and made them into reality, those that expanded their factories or made new ones, those that created new jobs, those that provide foodstuffs and goods that we need and buy, those that create new goods and services and bring them to the market. In other words, we criticize those who create wealth and wellbeing, as if they had done a bad thing to everyone else.

No good, nor precious stones, nor any raw material that is found in nature, can generate wealth by itself or give wellbeing to anyone. The only thing that creates wealth and wellbeing is the creative worker.

Gold and precious stones are important only when people, who through their own effort and work have bettered themselves already exist, people that created and possess goods, and now can give themselves the luxury of exchanging part of those goods or wealth, food, clothing, home, etc. for things like gold or precious stones that almost only serve to be looked at or to sparkle. And even so, one has to work so that they shine.

For those primitive people in the above example, had we found them stepping on gold and playing with diamonds, would the jewels have been able to help them increase their quality of life and come out of poverty? They could not have benefited from them at all, until the day that people who possessed wealth arrived and offered to exchange the gold and the diamonds for things that could indeed help them: those insignificant hooks and lines for fishing, or saws, nails, and hammers that would help them to make better houses, or needles and thread for sewing, or seed to plant. And most importantly, to teach them to work, along with the advantages of efficiency, will, and constancy.

Wealth is not distributed; wealth is created. And it is created through work, above all if it is accompanied by good ideas, constancy and the desire to overcome. And if we want wealth to come for others, we never create obstacles for those who create wealth, but rather on the contrary, we should facilitate their progress, always having in mind that those that progress are precisely those that create wealth and well-being. That we earn much more by teaching he who has nothing to work and produce, than taking from those who make wealth in order to give to those who produce nothing. And instead of criticizing those who create wealth, we should hail them as examples to others. And encourage them and decorate them so that they multiply, and so develop more people generating wealth and wellbeing by learning from their work, their organization, their ideas and experiences.

Never, then, do we make obstacles for those who create wealth because it is like denying to others – above all to the most needy– prosperity and wellbeing. And always keeping in mind that it is one thing for people to give spontaneously and voluntarily of what is theirs, and a very different thing to obligate them to give.

Let us do away, then, with the myth of the distribution of wealth. We achieve nothing living at the expense of others. We all are under the obligation to overcome our circumstances. We can achieve many things when there is interest and will, and when work, effort, and sacrifice are always rewarded.

But we refer to the true creators of wealth. To those that made themselves by their own effort and sacrifice. Unfortunately now there are many millionaires that are not true businesspeople or creators of wealth. They created ill-had money, and the majority are figureheads of those that "justify all means to achieve their ends." Let us be cautious of them.

IS IT POSSIBLE TO ELIMINATE CAPITALISM?

Capital exists in all systems of government. And it will still exist even in the most perfect systems of government that may come in the future. Because in every country goods or wealth exists that man has created in his desire to overcome, and each one of those goods has a value: that which we assign it by comparing it to others. And each one or summed together, this is what we call capital. What we want to clarify is that: capitalism will not be eliminated in any way, that it will always exist, but that it can change hands. For this reason, what is important is to know in what way the population is benefitted more and in what way people have more liberty and are less subjected: if under the direction or administration of its own creators, inheritors, or previous proprietors or under the direction of those who take this capital in order to monopolize it in the hands of one person or in one political party.

We repeat, whether it is called capital, goods, or property, it exists in all countries in the world. The radical difference: in whose hands they can be found. Who has them at their disposal? Who administers them? Who are really its owners? If it is distributed among millions of people, what we call private capital (examples: the United States, Mexico, and Canada), or if it is monopolized, meaning in the hands of one or very few people, be it the State, the party, or Fidel (example: the Cuban case, although there are also many countries with mixed capitalism, where many businesses or services are monopolized by the State). In this case what is important is to know in what way the population benefits more, meaning: which businesses give better prices, which give better service, which pay their employees and workers better, which pay more taxes and which progress more, if those that the State monopolizes or those that are in private hands and competing against one another. And this is easy to know, comparing the prices and the quality of service that some businesses give, comparing the prices and the quality of

61

service that some state businesses in Europe give, that they be self-sufficient and have no government help – with similar private businesses in the United States. And this study can be done – if they haven't already done it – by any university, or any other information or opinion outlet, which is truly concerned with the wellbeing of the people.

In the countries with a free market and free enterprise system, the State is limited by taxes to obtain sufficient funds for the execution and maintenance of public works: parks, highways, etc. It is limited to taxation to watch over the education, health, and security of all, and to provide social assistance for those who need it. In this case, the proprietors of businesses keep the larger part of the profits in order to use them for what they consider most convenient, because obviously, they are the ones who know the inherent problems of their business best.

In contrast, the opposite occurs in countries where the businesses and capital are monopolized by the party or the "State." The more they try to make people believe that goods or capital belong to the people, in practice it will always belong to those that posse and decide everything having to do with capital. Meaning that, contrary to what many people are made to believe, instead of being distributed, capital is concentrated in fewer hands, among fewer people, and probably in inept hands. At the end of the day, those who direct and decide everything about capital, whatever they are called, in practice are the sole owners and proprietors of that capital.

Capital, then, cannot be eliminated in any way. What it can do is change hands. Either it can be distributed among millions of people, generally in the hands of its creators, inheritors, or later buyers, or it is in the hands of those that hold power.

WHERE IS THE MOST PEOPLE LIVING IN POVERTY?

One characteristic of the domineering Marxist regimes is that they reduce man to the category of domestic animals like the horses or camels that we raise for work and competition. Or like the cow and hens that we raise so that they give us what serves as our nutrition. Or like the dogs, that we also feed, take care of, and teach many things, but always at our convenience and for our own benefit. Because the same thing that happens to our animals happens to people that live submitted to a leftist dictatorship: they are locked up and watched at all times. They are not permitted to emigrate or live where they please. They learn what their masters order them to or permit them to. Information or education they receive is in accordance with what the masters want them to see, read, or hear. They even ration their food, and they even have to resign themselves to the medications and the veterinary attention they are given. On top of all that, they are condemned for life to having to obey. For this class, the class of the eternally marginalized, it is really pure equality; everyone is poor, slaves to the system, and they lack the certainty of a better future because their future does not depend on their actions.

Where are there more poor people! Is it not in these totalitarian regimes where, excepting those sole owners or absolute masters of the country, everyone has to conform to being workers or employees of the governing class (the only rich people who provide everything that exists), while the people completely marginalized from politics and the media are condemned for life to be like the livestock in a farm to be and to do what the owner feels is convenient?. Is it not precisely in these countries where there are more poor people? Is this the equality that the enemies of free enterprise want: that everyone is poor, slaves of the system, and without a hope for a better life?

But it is good to note that everything has its advantages and disadvantages: that in democratic countries with a free enterprise system, because the people are at complete freedom, they are more enthusiastic and entrepreneurial than those that live in those countries where all the means of production are in the hands of a few. But we should also say that life in the free countries is more stressful, because each person has to worry about his future. In contrast, in the leftist dictatorships, the responsibility falls on the functionaries. The problem is that the functionaries worry more about themselves, while the people remain with their hands tied, enduring all kinds of hardships. All of this is of great importance when we are considering the political system that brings the greatest amount of wellbeing and happiness to people.

On the other hand, in all countries, and no matter the system of government, all occupations should necessarily exist -- from administrators, engineers, doctors, mechanics, nurses, and farmers, even the most indispensable workers. Unfortunately not everyone can be a boss, because in order to be the boss, one must have people to order around, they must have subalterns, and these subalterns are the majority. I mean that in every country, no matter the political system, someone has to carry out the work of the lesser rank. It is not possible to avoid. We wanted to clarify that point because many imagine an egalitarian world without subordinates and without bosses, and this is impossible. What is important is that each person is respected because of his or her equal fundamental rights. That everyone can communicate freely his ideas to his fellow men without the interference of anyone. That all people have the opportunity for study and to overcome their challenges, and that the differences between people are made by their own limitations or capacities. That everyone can work doing what they like, provided they are capable of earning a living by doing it. And that everyone is sheltered by a good social security, like that which exists in developed countries that are respectful of private property, and where even the workers at the lowest level live better than those who live submitted to totalitarian leftist regimes.

IS IT POSSIBLE TO ELIMINATE POVERTY?

Because of movies or televised reports that show people in developing countries rummaging through piles of trash, possibly to make us believe there is a great deal of poverty, it is necessary to clarify the following: in a society where all can and have the freedom to do with their life what they wish, it will be very difficult not to find people living in miserable conditions for the simple reason that they prefer it, or they make their living by being in that condition. We refer to individuals that because of life circumstances have given into or let themselves be defeated by drugs or alcohol, and they are rejected, not only by their families, but rather by all of society. And although institutions have been created to help these people return to a normal life, there are always new ones that fall into vice, or have a relapse, and add themselves to those who did not accept help. To those we must add the vagabonds and beggars that prefer to live in this way, be it because they do not like those who are in charge, or because they do not like to work. What we want is to clarify, that while the system lets them live this way, even if they live in a country where the means of production and service are in the hands of a small few or in one where the means of production are in the hands of millions of proprietors, there will always be people who prefer to live in this way. And that the only way to not see these people, is prohibiting them from living this way, and obligating them to work, as some leftist totalitarian regimes do. Although in this way they loose the sacred right of living as they want to, be it begging for alms or collecting leftovers in trash heaps. This is the case in the United States. It is a question of deciding by popular vote what is preferable: obligating them to work but losing a fundamental right or letting them live the way they want and being ignored by the media. But we also should say that if in countries with regimes similar to that of Cuba, they had permitted looking for food in trash heaps, surely no one would try it because they know beforehand that it is a waste of time, because they will find nothing.

WHAT HAPPENS TO THE PROFITS OF BUSINESSPEOPLE?

Let us see what happens with the money of the people that earn a lot in free market countries with free enterprise systems. Let's think about Don Antonio, who has a large business with which he earns a lot of money. What does he do, or what could this man do with all this money? In the first place, he cannot go without food, but he does not have more than one mouth, one stomach, one body and he will not eat more than other people generally eat. And at times even less, because, as all mortals, he also gets sick or goes on a diet. Will he burn the bills lighting tobacco as some cartoon pictures describe them? Not even then could he cause harm to anyone, because as we all know, one only needs paper to replace the bills, and in addition, all of those bills end up burned when they are old. But lets get to the heart of the matter. What can Don Antonio do with all that money that his business produces? If he were in a country with a regime like the Cuban one, where capital is managed by the small group that holds power, probably the business would not have made a profit, and in the case that it did, the profits would pass to the banks and there the party planners decide its destiny. In a country with a market and free enterprise system, the profits of Don Antonio also go to the bank, and there they only have one alternative: to produce, because naturally the banks should not have the money lay idle because of the losses they would incur, so they should put it into circulation, they should make it produce. And if Don Antonio did not reinvest the money, because he was sick, weary, or frustrated with the bad politics that only see him as an exploiter, it will be the banks that will have the task of distributing it in loans of all types to medium, large, or small-scale businesspeople who will start out enthusiastically with great aspirations. Naturally, it is probable that because of the inexperience or incapability of some of these businesspeople, a part of the money cannot achieve its mission, but in any

67

case the money is distributed, thus completing its social labor.

And if things go well politically in the country, and no one puts an obstacle in the way of those that want to grow and prosper, it will probably be the same Don Anonio with his demonstrated experience and capacity and with the help of the people he has confidence in, who want to reinvest the money, by expanding his business or founding other new ones that evidently will generate more jobs, more goods or foodstuffs, or more services that people need or that are scarce in the market. It is people like Don Antonio that create progress in the whole world. They are the great creators of wealth and wellbeing, as much in developed countries as in developing countries. And we also should say that usually they are those who have a better organization and those that pay their employees and workers better. It is these people who we should admire, encourage, or imitate, and not on the contrary criticize them or imagine them as ogres who are enemies of the popular classes, as we see that the enemies of private property, with their relentless disinformation and propaganda tell us. It is people like Don Antonio that benefit all of humanity because their progress translates to wealth and benefits for all. And the more businesses they have, they will not take the bread from other people, but rather on the contrary, by expanding them or founding other new ones, they will generate more food, more jobs, and more goods and services, which is precisely what makes progress, abundance, and reduction of the cost of living. It is people like Don Antonio, the great creators or riches and wellbeing, and of which we should say also benefit the enemies of free enterprise, and probably even more than their own creators and proprietors. In addition, we all die, and these great men do also, but the businesses remain there producing and ennobling the country and the world to the benefit of all. And let us not be so selfish as to look down on them when they travel or buy residences or luxury vehicles. Are these not the things that encourage us most to work, create, and produce? And these monies that are spent on commodities are they not equally serve a social purpose, by giving work and food to other people who also need to work and eat?

THE CREATIVITY OF THE FREE MAN

We all know the millions of products that are sold in stores and supermarkets. And every day more come out. And we can say that they all are born of private initiative. It will be very difficult to find products on the market whose invention we owe to the enemies of private business. These products, just like the people or businesses that produce them, we would not have known if it were not for the initiative and the efforts of everyday people that try to overcome, that try to improve economically, that try to make money, and above all strive to be important. And this is very difficult to achieve in the countries with totalitarian leftist regimes. Because what interest would the party or the state have in creating or inventing a new type of shampoo, bologna, sauce, paper, soft-drink, or vehicle. All of these products through the years were coming out on the market, we accustomed ourselves to them, and now many of them are indispensable to us. And we can even be so accustomed to them that we never stop to think that before they did not exist. But, even primary products like sugar or wheat flour, are for sale because of private initiative. They exist because someone thought of the refining process to make them more pure and long-lasting, and in putting them for sale in the market as a form of making money and becoming someone important. If these private initiatives had not existed we would still be crushing sugar cane to obtain a little bit of juice, because even the sugar mill and the paper mill are also the fruit of private initiative. Or we would be cleaning wheat or corn with our hands on our primitive houses. And we say that because the infinity of materials and tools that today are indispensable to make a modern house, like the variety of blocks, cements, glass, rods, wood, ceramics, Formica, paints, cable and tubes of all types. The products created and invented by man in his desire to overcome are millions, because of his desire to be known, to make money, and to feel important. And all products were unknown until the moment in which their creators introduced them to the market.

70

It is the free man to whom we own the existence, variety, and quality of all the things that we use and consume today, like almost all of the inventions and modern technological advances. It is also the free man to whom we owe the existence and variety of services, like the invention of almost all sports, games, and entertainment. And every day more come out. In contrast, what product, what service, or what sport of those that we buy, use, or play today was created or produced by the closed Marxist regimes?

CONSUMERISM

All the commodities that we have today we owe to free men who wanted to be different than others, who tried to overcome their challenges. They looked for a way to give themselves commodities. And when they had them, logically they became unequal with the rest.

And they continue inventing things for their wellbeing. However, in Marxist dictatorships, incapable of producing them, they encountered a word to criticize everything that they invented and sold in free countries, and they called it by the name "consumerism." They want us to see them as things that were missing from our lives. The manipulation and the campaign of discrediting them that they waged were such that even the Pope himself in the Vatican criticized "consumerism." This makes us think that if the Marxists had installed themselves throughout the whole world, chairs had not yet been invented, we would still probably be sitting on the floor or in the branches of trees, because all new inventions have been part of consumerism. Do you imagine the enormous inequality of someone on their tremendous chair and the rest without anything? Perhaps there would not have been consumerism that had wanted to make and sell them? Probably they would have confiscated it in order to avoid inequality and consumerism. But the same happens with everything; no one ever wanted an air conditioner until the first were invented, we accustomed ourselves to them, and today they are indispensable. Let us remember very well when the first cell phones came out. We even read a prominent article in the principal newspaper of the city criticizing these artifacts and their first users. We could swear the person who wrote that article today possesses at least one of the latest models, and he really did need it. Our brothers who stayed behind only need food. Because, certainly, these other things we only need after we have accustomed ourselves to them. For this reason new commodities, large or small, for the left would have been consumerism. So it was good that the enemies of private property did not come to install themselves throughout the whole world, because they would have done away with consumerism, or in other words, with progress and the evolution of man.

And in order to realize how they manipulate us through the media: since the Chinese became the first exporters of non-essential products, thanks to western investors and the return of Hong Kong by the English, now they talk very little of consumerism.

PAID WORK

Which was first, the chicken or the egg? In truth: no one has been able to know the true answer, if it was the egg so that the chicken could hatch or the chicken so that it could lay the egg. The same occurs when we try to guess who invented paid work. Or who had the initiative, if it was the worker or the employer. Or when we try to find out which of the two benefits more from it. Or who needs the other more, the worker or the proprietor. However, it is probable that it is the workers that the employer needs more, because there is a great quantity of small businesses or companies attended to by the same proprietor and his family, and this type of business, if it is obliged to stay that way, can subsist without problems. But those people that lack ideas to arrange things for their benefit, depend more on someone who can offer them a job. What we can be sure of is not that, until the day that the first paid work was done, no salaried worker existed nor did the employer. One of the parties had the initiative. Had there not existed an agreement between the parties, they would not have been able to carry out the first day of paid and voluntary work. And these voluntary agreements between the employer and worker can only be made at the moment that one of the parties sees how he will benefit.

Let us suppose that you have a small business of buying and selling in your own home. And you, yourself, take charge of the buying and selling. You had never been an employer. And as you do not have workers, neither did you have to worry about pay and salaries, nor about whether they arrived late or missed work, or can steal merchandise for themselves. You like your job, and can open and close the business at the time that you want. You think about it, see the opportunity to help him and also to take advantage of your time for more important things, and for this reason you hire him to see how it will turn out. Here we see the beginning of a work relationship, a job that is paid. Now then, does the fact of you agreeing to employ a person mean that you are going to exploit him or that you are going to damage him in some way? Who needs whom more? Could both not come out having benefitted?

Now, let us suppose that business is going well and you decide to expand: you look for an appropriate site, you get a loan from the bank in order to get what you need (with a guarantee of your house), and you employ more people. You start a small business where everyone should be benefited: your workers with a permanent job, the clients who are satisfied with a good service and good prices, and you with additional profits that, in addition to increasing your quality of life, could serve you, like every ambitions person, to continue expanding your business, and perhaps even convert it into a great chain of department stores. Well now, have you damaged society? Are the workers not those who have benefited the most? Did they not need you more than you needed them? You and your idea are benefitting many people: giving work to people that did not have it, benefiting the population by giving a quality service, and contributing to the prospering of other businesses with the buying power that your workers now have, and with that of your own business that needs to provide itself with merchandise, equipment, supplies and everything that is necessary for the service that you provide. In conclusion, you are a great benefactor. And before, you lived a calmer life attending personally to your business, until you got this idea in your head of placing this great burden and responsibility on your shoulders: of being the only one that worried about the problems and the debts of the business, you many times did not sleep, and even compromised your health. In contrast, your employees complied with your work schedule and went home without worry. It is probable that the worker needs the employer more than the employer the worker. However, many times we hear that the employer is benefiting himself from the workers. However, everything depends on who the employer is: if it is the State or the Party, they benefit their workers, despite they have them enslaved. But if it is private, the owner is the only one benefited and the workers are exploited, it does not matter if they work less, earn more, and are more content with their work.

"SURPLUS VALUE"

Marx pointed out that surplus was the difference that existed between the value of the goods produced and the salaries that the workers received for producing them, and that this difference was taken by the owner for himself. It is that simple. He did not take note of the large variety of circumstances that come into play so that the surplus can be produced, or in other words so that profit can be produced.

Today, it is more than demonstrated that the quantity of work necessary to produce a good is unequal in all places, depending on the brain that directs the means and the form of production. Whether surplus exists or not depends equally on efficiency and the mode of production.

But we do not only have to seek efficiency and workers performance to get some type of surplus; we also have to avoid wastes of raw materials, the use of inadequate material or products, breaking of equipment, the loss of utensils and tools, and an infinity of details that make saving money possible in order to be able to achieve a surplus. In the same way we have to try to achieve quality in what is produced to gain the confidence of the consumer. Although this is more generalized in free market and free enterprise countries, or rather in the countries where competition exists. Because in those countries where the State monopolizes production, people do not have another alternative than to be content with the products they can get, or what the State offers them. Obviously, this means a worse quality of life for the people that live in Marxist dictatorships and better quality of life for the people that live in countries with a free enterprise system.

Surplus is also what permits the business to grow, invest in new equipment in order to modernize, produce a larger quantity of goods and services, to carry out research, to give a business adequate maintenance, and to create new jobs to satisfy the requirements of the population. But the most

77

important thing in terms of achieving a surplus is organization and coordination.

Be they private or State-run, in whatever of the cases, the businesses should obtain surpluses if they want to provide to the population the necessary foodstuffs, goods, and services, and increase the supply of work because of the increased population. If the surplus was distributed amongst the workers, the businesses would not progress, they would stagnate, and in the end they would fail. Because when the needed increase of goods and services does not exist, this gives way to scarcity, lines and rationing, precisely what occurs in totalitarian Marxist regimes, despite the minimal growth of the population, caused by the imposition of severe demographic controls as the most simple form of taking care of the scarcity of foodstuffs, goods, and services.

For a business to progress, and with it the country where it is located, there should necessarily be a surplus. This was precisely the case in those countries where expropriations, nationalization or confiscation of businesses were made where we could all observe, not only that these countries' businesses lacked a surplus, but also that they were converted into a burden for the contributors by maintaining these businesses with their taxes, among others, while the countries having the private businesses that did have a surplus, had been able to use their taxes for new public works, or to improve the existing ones, or in social assistance, or in financing new industries for the increase in production.

Any person with the experience of founding a business and progressing along with it knows these realities and knows how important it is to have a profit or surplus.

IF IT IS GOOD FOR BUSINESS, IT IS EVEN BETTER FOR EMPLOYEES AND WORKERS

Some people think, or are made to believe, that when a measure that a government takes benefit businesses, it is bad for employees and workers. Or to benefit the poor we have to damage businesses. Fortunately things are not this way. As a general rule, when the measures are good for private business, they are better for the country and for the employees and workers because they benefit the most from these policies. Because by improving the economic conditions of the business, the conditions improve for growing, for increasing production, for sending cheaper products into the market, for improving the wages or increasing the number of workers, or for expanding or opening new branches, all of which will result in more jobs, better salaries, more production, more competition, more quality in what is produced, and automatically better quality of life. In contrast, when the measure hit the business sector, the employees and workers are the most hurt because of the contrary effect named previously, and because they probably have to dismiss workers, by which unemployment increases, production decreases, the country sinks into depression, conditions will not exist to increase the wages of those who deserve it, and crime can even increase as a consequence of unemployment and the high cost of living.

It is not necessary to go around the world to realize that when private enterprises prosper, everyone progresses, especially employees and workers. But when the measures damage it, the country sinks into depression and all of us suffer the consequences.

Some years ago, England passed through one of its worst crises: unemployment, inflation, fiscal deficit, and economic stagnation as a consequence of previous leftist governments that nationalized businesses, and applied higher and higher taxes in order to confront bigger bureaucratic costs. Until a woman arrived with her head on straight to put things in their place. Margaret Thatcher put value back again in England and was reelected as Prime Minister two consecutive times. And what was the extraordinary thing that she did? Precisely the opposite of what governments generally do, on one hand lowering taxes, so that more people had money to save or buy, and the investors had to invest and on the other hand privatized state businesses converting employees and workers into proprietors, decreasing the bureaucracy so that more people could carry out productive work. But England is not an isolated case. Almost at the same time, in the United States the same thing happened: high unemployment, inflation, and fiscal deficit, increase in interest rates, etc. a consequence of the populist government of Jimmy Carter, the only difference being that in this country, state businesses never existed. Ronald Reagan applied the same policy, on one end reducing taxes and on the other reducing bureaucratic costs. Reagan, in the same way, brought his country out of the recession and out of the dangerous process of inflation that was unfolding, and was even reelected.

And if the increase in taxes slows the economy of developed countries, what could we say of the developing countries that need the work and the increase in production much more?

Some seem to ignore, that if it goes well for those that produce and create jobs, it will go better for those that need those jobs and that production. It is natural. How could needy people get work or improve what they already have, if the people that could help them are also going through bad times. Could a country damage itself because people progress and acquire wellbeing as a consequence of their work and their ideas that at the same time bring wellbeing to others? Perhaps it is not economic growth of the people that makes the wealth of a country? If you have a sewing machine with which you make pants, and someone stops it from working, would you not produce fewer pants? In the same way, in the same measure, they impede progress and development. The intelligent thing to do is imitate the good result and shy away from that which has failed, and even more so in politics and the economy, where we all suffer the consequences. For example: if you observe two cooks that make cakes and desserts, and one's cakes come out good and the other's come out bad, which recipe would you choose when you had to make a good cake?

The most intelligent thing to do in order to help the neediest is to facilitate the production of that which he produces or wants to produce. For this reason, the best governments are the ones that help production.

Exaggerated taxes are another serious error: the bad government is the great predator that strangulates and asphyxiates all citizens making it difficult for them to grow and prosper. And even more serious when it does not distribute the basic services as it should, nor does it give adequate maintenance to the parks and highways of a country, nor does the necessary public works, because it prefers to take the government's revenues to other countries in order to disgracefully bring the revolution of misery to an international level (Chavez's way). In addition, we all know that taxes are never good, although we understand it is a necessary problem, but the less taxes the better.

CREATION OF WEALTH AT THE MACRO LEVEL

Another error, as common as that of the supposed distribution of wealth between people, is also committed at the macroeconomic level, when they try to make us believe that the existence of poor countries is to be blamed on developed countries.

For example, when inhabitants of a developed nation invest and bring part of their goods, equipment, materials, and qualified personnel to backward countries, be it to extract some mineral, or to install some factories, or to develop some agriculture, as was the greater part of the investments of the West in Africa and America, or more recently in Asia. After some time, when the country is in complete transformation and thousands of people have come out of poverty, the enemies of free enterprise begin to signal to the class differences among the population, not positively, but rather in a negative way. And instead of thanking the investors because of whom a large part of the population have overcome their poverty and now live better in comparison to how they lived before the arrival of the investors, pointed out on the contrary, on the differences of status as if these always had existed, wanting to make believe the most poor people, and even many who have improved their quality of live, to believe that they are not in better economic conditions because of the foreigners who came to exploit them. That they are poor because of the foreign investors and because of those who now live better (a category that includes the natives that improved and made their fortunes with the arrival of the investors). That they are poor because of those that now are no longer needy, and whose only sin was to work to overcome their circumstances, and help to create wealth.

And the supporters of free enterprise are blamed for everything. For as much wellbeing, progress, and comfort that they have generated, the enemies of free enterprise will always get something reproachable of which to accuse them.

82

They even blame them for altering or absorbing some primitive cultures (although perhaps, the only way of having avoided this interaction would have been leaving them to their fortune) for example, so that the African or American tribes continue as they had been for a thousand years, no government or outsider should even visit them, because they would be risking the transmission of diseases to them for which they were not prepared. It was only logical to maintain these differences, which are many, and which distinguish us better when the different cultures live separately but relatively equal in climate, land, and availability of water and natural resources. But when the cultures are united, as is the case in the colonization of Africa as much as America, the most developed absorbs the other, not so much by imposition, but rather by natural evolution, because no one tends to make things worse for themselves, but rather the contrary, all rational beings procure the greatest wellbeing, food security, prevention and cure for diseases, and protection for his family, but always conserving customs and traditions. These were precisely the changes that took place throughout the whole world when the colonizers mixed with natives in regions in which for thousands of years the natives lived a semi-savage life, in a constant fight against diseases, bad weather, insects, and the savage environment that was around them. And it is here in these countries, with difference cultures mixing themselves, where we can observe the complex process of evolution and change. And of how the most developed absorb the others, not so much by impositions, rather because each person seeks his own wellbeing. And it is in this process where we naturally observe among the population different qualities of life, but always with the primitive population living better than before. This integration and natural fusion could take hundreds of years, and it is during this evolutionary process where unhealthy political practices come into play to gain the favor of the less favored sectors, with well orchestrated campaigns of misinformation, blaming the most developed for the alteration of their cultures and trying to make the most unfortunate believe that they are so unfortunate because of those who live better than them. This was one of the most common and errant assertions supported by the left: blaming the most developed countries for creating poverty in countries that they called part of the Third World. Even the leftist intellectuals believed this. Among them there is a book with the title that says it all: "Open Veins of Latin America," an almost mandatory reading for students in our universities: a true compilation of hate toward North Americans and the English. With this book they taught the students of a supposed "economic bleeding" that the rich countries did to the poor ones, in addition to the apparent exploitation and economic dependence they caused. These were supposedly the causes of our problems, and it would be the enemies of free enterprise who took it upon themselves to correct them. Today we know very well the great error in which they were a part, and it is precisely the very leaders of these countries, who now exhaust all the springs to make the capitalists return as investors or to exploit and bleed their countries that are still backward as a consequence of years of stagnation. Today no one has a doubt that it is the proprietors and investors who create wealth and wellbeing. For this reason the current interest of the Marxists in persuading all the great capitalists to invest in their countries. However, by not clarifying these truths, and continuing to confuse the population and cause problems for countries with free enterprise, they show that they really do not desire a globally developed world without needy people, but rather, one world run by one master.

LIBERALISM AND NEOLIBERALISM

Let us not confuse Liberalism with Neoliberalism. Or let us not permit them to confuse us because when we see supposed "analysts" in the media, almost never do they refer to Liberalism, but rather to Neoliberalism, and in a derogatory way, because when they refer to it, they accompany it with the "savage" word, which is a contradiction: such savage Neoliberalism does not exist. It is called this precisely, because it is the modern form of liberalism that permits the intervention of the state as much in legal terrain as in economic.

For its part, we could indeed call liberalism savage. But it was not someone's invention. It is the natural form that people had, since they have existed on the earth, of changing or exchanging one thing for another, and by which they supported one another and by which all the countries that today we consider developed prospered.

The enemies of private property say of liberalism that the only ones that sacrificed themselves were the poor. With what easiness there are things distorted after some people do not live better than others! As if the rich of today were not precisely the poor of yesterday!

Economic liberalism or the free market was really the only system, that in relatively short time, was capable of creating sufficient wealth and wellbeing. Liberalism demonstrated its special capacity to elevate the standard of living of the people. Bolivar, a wise man who was witness in his time of progress in many countries said: "Society unrecognized those that do not procure general happiness, to him who does not busy himself to increase with his work, talents and industry his wealth and own commodities that collectively form national property." But let us not confuse liberalism with neoliberalism, because this is characterized by the interventionism of the State in economic relations that always existed between individuals, just as in the organization that they created. And it is precisely this interventionism, with the excessive bureaucracy or taxes, that which brought many countries into stagnation or to failure. Neoliberalism is a liberalism that has been intervened in, directed , and for this reason it is a tremendous error to refer to it as savage. And those that put up with it better are the developed countries, precisely for this reason, because they are already developed. But without a doubt, the less interventionism the better. History and experience teach us that the more liberal the economy of a country is, the faster the progress. We can observe this in the same leftist dictatorships when they open themselves up to private investment, to the free market and to free enterprise.

WHY ARE THERE STILL POOR COUNTRIES?

Some politicians overlook the fact that developed countries were also poor once and that it was not so easy to become what they are today. That there were many years that hardships and sacrifices had to be made, and long workdays that had to be worked, by even the smallest children of every family. Everyone had to do the work and make the necessary sacrifices to better themselves. And no one expected the state or other people had to maintain them. Development was only possible when each person or family group tried to satisfy their own needs.

Unfortunately in that time they could not avoid the period of hard work and discipline through which countries must pass in order to achieve general wellbeing.

Venezuela, like other Latino countries, also should be among the developed countries. The Venezuelans have had abundant economic resources, and more than sufficient time in comparison with the United States or Canada, and taking into account that the colonizers arrived first to South American lands. More than 100 years later the colonizers arrived at North American lands.

Things would be very different if our governors had had the political, disciplined and hard-working mentality that made these northern countries prosper.

It would probably be an error to lay the blame for our problems on our idiosyncrasies, on our very legitimate and joyful way of life. Let us remember that in this aspect the United States is the most heterogeneous country in the world. There are not just Anglo-Saxons, there are also a great percentage of Latinos, blacks, Indians, Asians and other races and mixes that exist. However, this was never an obstacle to progress and development. There the Latinos also demonstrated that they were hard-working, intelligent, and progressive, and that they could be as disciplined and organized as the rest.

Unfortunately in Venezuela and in many other Latin-American countries, above all in the last few decades, anti-capitalist, populist, and Marxist influences predominated. The results have been catastrophic. The same has occurred in other countries with the same populist experiences, very different from the liberal and hard-working culture that made developed countries prosperous.

And it has nothing to do with chance: We are poor because of the damages that the interference of the government in matters that did not concern them. We are poor because of the disdain for the fundamental moral and religious principles. We are poor because our work is made difficult by the introduction of terms like "exploitation" and "class warfare", fomenting hate, indifference, and conflict of workers with their bosses. We are poor because of the usurping of authority: instead of the public employees being at the service of the community, it is the community that is subjugated by them. We are poor because of the expropriation of the means of production that worked well in private hands, creating corruption of all types and dejection and unease among the working and progressive people. We are poor because of legal and personal insecurity, by fomenting public disorder, tolerating delinquency, and permitting invasions of fields and lands, and the fabrication of hovels, systematically violating the right to own property. We are poor because of the demoralization that they cause to the whole society with all its logical and damaging consequences. Because of obstructionism and the many costly bureaucratic processes, because of inadequate and exclusionary money exchange policies and because of successive and impoverishing devaluations. We are poor because of price regulation, because of the taxes and inflationary increases of wages and salaries, and because of all of the other obstacles that should concern those who have the initiative of wanting to make some project or idea a reality. But above all we are poor because of the destructive practice of the enemies of private property of justifying all the evils in the world in order to arrive at their ends, and the role of corruption in all aspects.

Unfortunately, our governors, many of them influenced by flawed populist totalitarian "teachings", never took into account the extraordinary examples and experiences of the countries that achieved progress and complete development with free market economies, and in complete freedom. For this reason, many countries continue in poverty, and millions of people are hungry and in need. We invite then to eliminate these unjust and criminal practices and those unfortunate "teachings" in our schools that for some time have been confusing those that later are protagonists of injustice and deplorable socioeconomic situations.

Venezuela, with immense economic resources, should be today a super-developed country, just like others such as Argentina, that before the arrival of Peron, was headed toward total development, until the populists, anti-capitalists, and Marxists arrived.

WHERE DOES THE EXPLOITATION OF MAN OCCUR TODAY?

Previously, in a world of scarce goods and foodstuffs, each person tried to work his hardest, and doing work was the only way of surviving. And this is how it has occurred throughout human history, just as there were good employers, there were also inconsiderate ones. The enemies of private property took advantage of this to blame all the employers for exploitation. From then on, exploitation has been associated with the free enterprise system. But it is because of the Industrial Revolution, formed precisely by free enterprise and private initiative, that an explosive increase in production was achieved that permitted a reduction of the work day and prohibited child labor, which definitively would not have been possible without the increase in production.

But today where does the true exploitation of man by man take place? From the point of view of the enemies of private property, the exploitation depends on if we work in a state enterprise or a private one. For example: if you work in a State business, where you work a lot and are paid very badly, that is not exploitation. But if you work in a private business, one can swear that you are being exploited, despite you may work less and they pay you more.

Fortunately we can still think, and logic tells us that a person is exploited when at work he cannot, or does not dare to protest. When he has to resign himself to the work and the wage that he is given. When in all the places that has to go to work, he will deal with the same owners, with the same patron and does not have another alternative to put up with and obey. A person is exploited when he has to comply with the conditions that his sole employer imposes. A person is exploited when in some way he is punished by his sole employer and does not have another alternative to put up with. A person is exploited when he does not have anyone to go to in order to protest. A person is exploited when all his life he is subordinated to his sole patron: be it called government, party, state, master, commander, or however he is called, that takes possession even of people who then have to obey. And in what countries and with which system does this occur? Is it not in the countries with totalitarian regimes where private property in the means of production and service does not exist? Naturally this obligates people to conform to the work and the wage they are given, to have to put up with the impositions of their sole employer, and to never protest because things will get worse for them. And who would like to stay his whole life submitted to that power?

How different it is when the means of production and services are spread out among millions of proprietors! How different it is when the worker seeks a better option and can demand and arrive at a private agreement with the patron!

Everyone knows that what is important is to be comfortable and content with the work, to be treated well, that you are taken into account as a person, that your effort is appreciated, and that this permits you to comply with the business goals or purposes. But this is very difficult to achieve in a regime where our destiny is decided by our masters, and our wellbeing depends on them, because they are responsible for giving each one his sustenance. Nor can we stop being workers or employees and become employers because we are not permitted to have our own businesses. And naturally, "there is not exploitation" despite we are unhappy with our work, with the treatment, with the pay, and with our sole employer.

How could a person be exploited while he has the freedom to choose his work, or to change his boss because he doesn't like the one he has, or to seek a better salary, or to manage his own business because he doesn't want to work for others and wants to be his own boss?

It is not that working for others is already exploitation. Why stop people from working for others if they want to, they enjoy it more and benefit more from it? Why stop them from making with their lives and their time what they want, provided they are not hurting others?

A person is exploited when they cannot change bosses despite not liking the one they have. A person is exploited when they know their work will not benefit their family, because their wellbeing depends on other's decisions. A person is exploited in their work, or outside of it, when they cannot complain. A person is exploited when he does not dare to demand a better treatment or a better salary. A person is exploited when he cannot freely leave the region where he lives. A person is exploited when he cannot give his children the education he wants, be it political or religious. A person is exploited when he is not permitted to start his own business. A person is exploited when he stops being a person and they convert him into an animal.

TODAY'S MASTERS AND SLAVES

We said on previous pages referring to equality that the very act of wanting to impose it causes even greater inequality among those who impose it and those who submit to it. Leftist governments divide people into two very different classes: the governing class, the modern masters that use an insolent power that naturally they never will want to give up in order to never have to obey, and the subjected class, the actual slaves, for whom it is very difficult to exit slavery, or in other words to access power. They produce the more extreme inequality and the worst distribution of wealth. And they made people believe that with the means of production in the hands of one party, of one government, or a tyrant, people will be less subjected and in better economic conditions? What a difference from the countries with free enterprise where wealth is distributed among millions of proprietors! And is not because of pure luck or chance, nor because someone distributed it amongst them, but rather because they themselves made it, inherited it or bought it. In contrast, in totalitarian Marxist regimes, these people took over by force the wealth of another and concentrated it in a smaller group, or with one sole proprietor. In contrast to what they proclaim, wealth is brought together in fewer hands, and generally in inept hands because they lack the capacity and the experience of their own creators, founders, inheritors, or previous proprietors. The working class is submitted and exploited by the all-powerful master (party, government or commander) that controls all and imposes all the rules that everyone has to obey.

And to be a slave it is not necessary to be whipped. In the new version, the mental punishment could be superior to the physical. By submitting their minds, they also enslave their bodies. It is the most absolute form of slavery: slavery of mind and body. People can even be made to commit suicide if the master wants it. It is what the terrorist leaders do with poor Muslims that put on their belt a bomb, or get them into a vehicle full of explosives and they command them to blow up alongside hundreds of innocent people.

This slavery can be worse that that of past years. Because the old slaves al least had alternatives: they were distributed between thousands of masters, all different, from the most despicable and unjust to the most generous and well meaning. They were subjected to the luck of the master that bought them. And when they got an unjust one, they had the hope of a change in masters, a very common occurrence, because things tend to go badly for the perverse, an outcome which slaves influenced by working reluctantly and for this reason they ended up being sold. Another difference between those masters and today's is that many believed in God and his commandments, and this obligated them to a more humane form of behavior. In addition, many wanted to feel appreciated by their slaves. In contrast, today's Marxist masters are atheists. They justify all evils in order to arrive at their ends. They are capable even of sacrificing their family, because what is important for them is to get and maintain power.

POWER TO THE PEOPLE?

Oh, how they manipulate people!

In the first place, in Marxist regimes the people do not have any power whatsoever over those who monopolize power, a monopoly which cannot be changed or punished. The marginalized class does not decide about the privileged class. In contrast, the privileged, the sole property owners decide the destiny and the future of the subjected: what they can read, what they can write, what they are going to learn, what they are going to hear, the movies and television shows that they can see, how and when they are going to live, what they are going to eat, and even who is going to live and who is going to die. It is the worst slavery. Forget my friend, that in this system, you may say to your boss or patron even about any complaint, unless you want a worse job than the first. How different is a country with a system of free enterprise! Where when the worker does not like the work, or the wage, or the treatment he is given, he can very well demand a change because he has infinity of places he can go, and of proprietors to whom he can go. And he also can be a boss or a proprietor. In contrast in the Marxist system of the exclusive and eternal proprietors, the workers will continue being workers, the employees will continue being employees and the privileged owners of capital and of people will continue being the only proprietors, no matter if they are terrible administrators, because, naturally, they themselves will not change things. And just as things have always occurred, they will continue to hold power.

One of the purported benefits of totalitarian Marxist regimes is that, supposedly, they teach all people to read and write. And why not, if when one is the owner even of the people, they can do with them whatever they want. They can even obligate them to teach each other. But of course, all learning must be done according to the instructions of the master. People have the same rights that horses and oxen have, when the master teaches them to pull the cart or plow well.

Another achievement attributed to these regimes is that supposedly healthcare is free. But the slaves were also given food and free healthcare. People are cared for in the same way the rancher feeds his animals, vaccinates them, and gives them veterinary assistance according to the potential benefit they give him. Just like our domestic animals, subjected persons in these regimes should become accustomed to what they are given, and to what their masters permit, They can only read, see, hear, or learn what is authorized by the regime, express what they are permitted to, and are forced to comply with the schedules and the work they are given. They cannot even choose a doctor they like, and should content themselves with the attention of the veterinarian they are assigned. People cannot make their opinions known publically unless they are in favor of the regime, nor can they criticize the masters of the system without fear of punishment. Much less can they protest in order to be set free and no longer be slaves. Because obviously, if freedom were to return, free expression would return and the publication of thoughts, which the masters don't like to read or listen to, nor do they like it that others listen to it as well. And they would have to listen to the supporters of free enterprise and of the most basic rights: like that of having the most determined and capable earning more and living better than the incapable and the lazy, or like that of having all people wanting to be different from the rest, and wanting to come out of mediocrity. Or of the right of all people to establish their own business, that really belongs to them, that no one can take away, that they can say out loud is theirs and can do with it what they want as long as they are not damaging others. To have the right to educate their children according to their own criteria, and not according to the criteria of a political party. Or to believe in God and in their religion, and to be able to teach it to their children. Or to live as they like and in the city or country they want to, as long as it does not cause damage to others. Because when man puts his effort into doing something and he does not have the masters blocking his path, it is almost certain that he will get it.

MICROENTERPRISE IN MARXIST DICTATORSHIPS?

One of the supposed final goals of Marxism, in addition to the inexorable subjection of people to the rules of a single Party, is that the means of production, service, opinion, and information pass to the hands of the "people," party, master, or governing group, all of which are actually the same thing. However, we see sometimes when leftists are in power in supposedly "democratic" governments, they make small loans to people of scarce resources for the promotion of microenterprises. Unfortunately, because of this constant practice of using and justifying all the means to arrive at their ends, we never know what their real intentions are, nor do we even know when they lie or tell the truth because they trick even one another. But suppose that there exists an honest proposal to create microenterprise, then we are tripped up by a contradiction: If the final goal of the enemies of free enterprise is that all enterprise is in their hands, why then do they excite humble citizens by making them believe that they can have their own businesses if the final destiny is to take them away when they consolidate their power? Do they ignore that the great majority of small, medium, and large companies that exist today in the world started as microenterprises (excepting naturally those made with ill-had money from official corruption)? Do they ignore the great sacrifices that new businesspeople have made including staying up all night and worrying in order to make progress and keep their new microenterprises afloat? Or do they recognize that when people work enthusiastically for themselves, and set a goal, for them a work schedule, holidays, and leisure time do not exist until they fulfill their purpose? Or will the future leftists officially permit private microenterprise? And if that were the case what would be the motive for not accepting the small and medium ones? And if they are also going to permit the holding of the small and medium private businesses what would be the motive for stopping those that become large businesses? Is it that the great sin of capitalism is that business progresses? Is it that when they grow, generating more consumer goods, more services, more jobs and better technology, they cause a great damage to the people and to the economy of a country? What reasons could the economists, sociologists, and ideologues who are enemies of free enterprise have for stopping a small business from employing more people, producing more, and making itself a big company? And if we know that the large businesses pay more to their employees and workers and even give better benefits, why then this fear of large businesses and their proprietors? And then what would be the size limit, capital and number of employees, for a business to grow to? In what moment should the growth be slowed down or expropriated? Or is it that the leftists are only going to permit those microenterprises whose only employee is the owner himself, or when more than his wife and children, if he has any and they are in the condition to work? And if they really are not going to permit every the smallest private business why then to they excite the humble citizens making them believe that they will have their own businesses if their final end is to take them away? And how then could the country prosper? Perhaps the masters could procure us infinity of jobs that daily offer us the free creative and entrepreneurial spirit that we all have inside us? Could a wide variety of small, medium and large businesses exist that today make up the developed countries and the developing ones of having stopped the proletariat from realizing their personal dreams? Is it that the leftists realize that the proprietors of today were precisely the poor of the past that did not want to continue being employees or workers? Would the progress of the whole world not be much more difficult if we all were provided with employment or a job? What country in the world could better itself or develop with the party as the only owner, boss, and employer? Would progress exist in the world today if 150 years ago we had globally installed Marxist totalitarianism? Perhaps it is not ambition or personal betterment that makes the greatness of a country? Is it not precisely the free enterprise system the only one that has demonstrated being capable of creating wealth, promoting well-being, and elevating the standard of living of the people? Is it so difficult to recognize the poor of yesterday for their ideas, constancy, and hard work that they had to do to get to where they are today? What reasons could exist for denying people the right to possess what they achieved with their work and with their saving, if by seeking their own well-being they also helped achieve prosperity for others. What was the cause of the failure of all the countries that made incursions into totalitarian Marxism, if not precisely stopping the proletariat from trying to better itself? Do they imagine living in a world where the sole owner, patron, and employer is the all-powerful party? Why it is so difficult for them to recognize the achievements of yesterday's poor who pulled themselves up by their efforts? Why be against the poor trying to better themselves? Could we all be forced to live perennially with what the state can give us? What interest could the people have in progress knowing they are condemned forever to be workers or employees of the only masters or proprietors? Perhaps we lack a study of developed countries and their distinguished businessmen in order to know that they were poor and how hard they had to fight.

We can affirm that in the last two centuries, the existing rivalry between these two systems has damaged us enormously. One is very aggressive, using any means in order to impose itself as it sees fit, and the other has very few mourners wanting to survive.

FROM THEORY TO PRACTICE

If we put submission on the side (which is more than sufficient to slip away from the enemies of free enterprise), and supposing that in the economic aspect they were to have obtained good results, there would not be so many reasons to fear them. Because even, with time, the most favored could be the same people that generally come out ahead in the free market and free enterprise system and become proprietors of the means of production and services. And we say generally, because today there are many millionaires that are not true businessmen, but rather figureheads of the left that buy businesses with misbegotten funds. We repeat, if in practice the means of production and services were to work well in the hands of a political party, the most favored could be all of those that in countries with free enterprise make great effort to succeed, as the most reliable and safe form of bringing about a better standard of living for his family, without being dependent on the benevolence of those that represent the party or the supposedly protective and paternalistic State.

And why do we say that they would be the most favored? Because they are the people that worry most about their economic security. For this reason they made and still make great efforts to succeed and leave mediocrity behind. For this reason, millions of people have achieved it, and for this reason many more continue trying.

If totalitarian leftist regimes really worked, how good would it have been for all of those people that worked and still work more than what is normal and by their own efforts and worry achieved a stable life and a future free of hardship! How good would it have been for those people, those that because of their own worries and efforts to move ahead became sick or aged prematurely! How good would it have been for those people that because of their sleepless nights, anguishes and worries about improving the conditions of their lives, died or did not get to enjoy the fruits of their

101

labor! Many of these people are creators of goods and services that today we enjoy.

And it is because of the system of free enterprise's own uncertainty that it is that people are more anguished, worried, made sick or even die earlier. Although we should recognize that this uncertainty or uneasiness is what made them be creative, by exercising the maximum effort to create new means of productions and of service, by establishing new industries and commerce, and by introducing new products to the market. Products that, incidentally, today we see as the most normal of things, but that surely would not have existed if not for the uneasiness of these people. In contrast, in a Marxist system that works well, they would not longer have to be worried about their well-being. How good it would be for these people and for the whole world if the state and the party could provide them (just like the free enterprise system) with everything they could ever need! Not only to live in the way they would like, but also to continue realizing the projects in mind, and those that in the future they might think of. Then, no, they would not have to worry about their futures, nor about their security and well-being as they did when they were starting out in order to get and keep a good job, nor by working overtime to get additional money and to be able to save in order to do their projects. Nor would they suffer from the fear of failing and being ruined.

Naturally, with a change of system, what worries all these people that slaved away and put in so much effort, is the uncertainty of their future. It worries them, with good reason, that the Marxists in all countries where they installed their dictatorships were not capable of satisfying the minimum needs of the population. It worries them, and with good reason, that after so much effort, because it was the only way of assuring a better future for themselves, they would be those who suffer the worst under the Marxists. It worries then, and with good reason, that after many prolonged sacrifices in order to live better, everything will collapse. That after a whole life of hardship in order to rise above, everything will fall apart because of people that ignore the well-being that they generated, for thanks to them there were sufficient foodstuffs, goods, and services, from which, incidentally, the leftists also benefitted.

They have to worry that after having worked for a better life, we will have to conform in the future with the little that those who created nothing give them, or that they want to give them.

It worries them and with good reason: That their rights and goods are usurped, they being those who deserve to have more than the rest. The creators are those that contributed the most to the well-being of others, yet they might be the most affected. That they will be stopped from benefitting from the fruits of their effort and work, while those that did nothing, enjoy the benefits of the work of someone else.

Of course it would be very good if the state were capable of providing all citizens with sufficient goods and services. And better still if that were done in complete liberty. Because let us not forget that in liberty, however insignificant a person seems, he could achieve extraordinary things. For this reasons free countries prosper, because when people do not have official obstructionism, they devise ways to achieve what they want.

Of course it would be very good if the totalitarian leftist regimes could supply us with everything just like the free countries can. But meanwhile, who is going to guarantee us that we won't pass through hardships, and that we will get everything that is necessary to live equally with those in free countries? For example: A pet, and its food, accessories, and medicines. Or a boat with all its implements for fishing or recreation.

If this system really worked, and in it people were free, we should be happy because many things would be

103

simpler for us. We could no longer have to worry about our futures, nor about working overtime, nor about staying up all night thinking about how to alleviate yesterday's problems. Nor could we have to worry about accounting, or taxes on the rent. It would be the functionaries of the party who in the future, supposedly, would worry not only about themselves, but also about everyone else. It would be the functionaries that were responsible that the people were not in need, and perhaps also the most affected, because they were accustomed to living without worries in capitalist countries, with very secure jobs, earning good salaries, getting all that they wanted, and without worrying about saving or putting anything aside. Now that the left has installed itself, that of which they were so sure, the system will charge itself with giving them whatever is necessary. For this reason they enjoyed everything they could. They were so accustomed to what is good in the system, that they even bought as much as they could, in complete liberty.

And as we are not sure of what really will occur, let's hope that God gets ahold of us after we've confessed.

SOCIAL BENEFITS

What people that are favored with new social benefits will not want them and support them? And the more people benefit from them, the more favorable they will seem to those who benefit. Does this mean then that the best governments are those that offer the most benefits? It would be very easy then to be a good governor, or a good legislator: One would only have to propose all the social benefits one could.

Unfortunately, social benefits do not make a country prosperous. And they can also be damaging. Unsuitable governments know this very well.

Social benefits could be very good, but they also could damage the economy of a country and end up being damaging for everyone.

This is because the prosperity of a country is only possible with the work and effort of people who try to satisfy their own family's needs. Only after that, can some benefits be proposed and implemented.

In many developed countries very good benefits have been achieved. But sometimes it happens that many people, with much reason, do not agree with some of these benefits because they consider them to be unjust or unnecessary and because their taxes pay the cost of them and there is damage to the economy as a consequence. This is the case with unemployment benefits when they are paid over a long period of time. Those who contribute complain that they also support those who simply don't like to work. They also complain that the government takes money to give education to those who could very well pay for their own studies, or those that do not value their education or take advantage of the opportunity the way they should. Or to maintain those that still being in the most productive state of life, are obligated to retire early, despite having their maximum amount of knowledge and the desire to continue being active.

105

This is the case for officers in the Armed Forces in many countries. The damage is double: strategic because of the retirement of valuable officers, and economic because they are replaced and have to continue being paid their pensions. The same happens with teachers and university professors who retire when they have more knowledge and experience to teach, without taking into account their physical and mental condition and the desire to keep working. Naturally this is most counterproductive in countries that are developing. And although some countries do not have problems financing these wastes because of the flow of dollars that they receive because of petroleum sales, others must increase taxes or create new ones that reduce the capacity for savings and investment. Then the damage is double: for those who they take from, investment and progress is made difficult and to those that receive them they become accustomed to it, which, if there is a bad situation, they prolong it or worsen it, because these benefits are unproductive. Firstly, we have to try to achieve a greater development so that more and better businesses exists, and so count with a greater number of contributors and more money to finance these benefits.

Unfortunately development is not made by decree, much less by robbing resources to finance revolutions or failed ideologies, nor by taking money with taxes from those that want to grow and progress, for bureaucratic wastes or in projects that could prolong the situation or make it worse. It is difficult to avoid the period of much work, discipline and sacrifice for those that countries should pass in order to arrive at general well-being. For this it is important to take into account the experiences of countries that develop in a relatively short period of time, that were equally poor, and that thanks to the effort of everyone, progress, and now enjoy good social benefits. We should have in mind that free enterprise as much as financial resources that people come to gain are indispensible to growth. That the more the government takes from those that produce, the more difficult it is to achieve development, well-being, and productivity that everyone wants. And when politicians ignore these fundamental economic principles it is very easy for them to make the situation worse.

WHO DIRECTS THE INVASION OF LANDS AND THE CONSTRUCTION OF SHACKS OR SHANTY TOWNS?

For more than fifty years we have observed in Venezuela and in other countries what has been called Agrarian Reform. And although many could think of this as something just that benefits the country and many people, this is not the case because it is done compulsively, by people who make believe that it is the rural people that take the initiative of invading and disrespecting property. And what very well could be done in perfect peace and without damaging the country or the proprietors, and even with important achievements, they have converted it all into a disaster.

Everyone knows that to realize a project with success, one must first plan and organize one's self.

How could we construct a building without plans, without calculations, with whatever material, on an alien terrain while we are fighting with the owner? And this is the Agrarian Reform as we have seen it in Venezuela and in many other countries.

How many fields are there in Venezuela that at one time produced, and that today would be prosperous businesses producing grain, fruits, meat, milk, and generating employment? Unfortunately, many of these fields were invaded and later abandoned, and this has been an economic burden for the nation. This type of "Agrarian Reform" is an obstacle to development, slows down investment in rural areas, and takes away the enthusiasm not only of farmers and ranchers, but also of those that are dedicated to other activities, but that equally note the serious absence of authority, order and discipline that should characterize a good government. When the producer does not feel safe, protected and respected in his ownership of the land, the incentives that are put into practice are of very little value.

What is really important: that the land is divided without taking efficiency into account, causing scarce productivity and a low quality of life of the smallholders (parceleros), or the efficiency, productivity and the high standard of living of the workers and employees that work in the large agricultural businesses in developed countries? Who lives better, the members of agricultural Russian, China or Cuba, or the workers and employees of the large private agricultural enterprises in the United States, Canada, or Europe? When did lands need to be redistributed in these countries? In addition, we should keep in mind that in the countries where private property is respected, the land is distributed equally in a natural way through the years: Every time a proprietor of a large tract of land dies, ordinarily his land is divided amongst his heirs, and some sell their share, and every once in awhile a landowner dies. However, if they still want to redistribute land to true farmers without damaging the economy of the country, first they should plan it out. But never on lands that already produce. Preferably in good lands that are unoccupied and concentrated as much as possible to lower costs and facilitate their organization. And in the case that the lands do belong to someone, the occupants or proprietors should first be compensated. Only after that is done, should then be distributed. They should keep in mind that the disrespect for the other drives dejection, corruption, disorder, impunity, laziness, and the most serious: the shortage of supply, principal cause of inflation. How could a country produce its own food without first doing away with this savagery that for so many years has damaged and delayed agricultural activity in Venezuela and in many other countries? How could we produce our own food without first bringing about confidence, encouragement and enthusiasm for the rural producers? Perhaps this is innate in civilized people to tolerate or incite inappropriate takeover of public or private goods? We should also say that the rural people are not to blame. The blame for the damages that they do to the country goes to the governments that permit these invasions in complicity with those who want to invade.

Unfortunately, in all countries where, because of populist influences, private property is not respected and invasions of fields and lands is tolerated or brought about, production decreases. These are the causes of famines in many countries, while in others there is scarcity and inflation, caused precisely by the arrival of leftist governments that are enemies of private property in the means of production. Today unfortunately this is made more serious by the nefarious increase of petroleum prices.

THE PROPRIETOR: A SIMPLE ADMINISTRATOR

We should look at the proprietor as he really is: a simple administrator of one of the goods that in practice belong to everyone, because we all benefit from it. Even after death, everything that the proprietor has founded and developed keeps on producing and benefitting everyone.

The mere act of rising and progressing by his own effort is the best test that he knows how to administrate and create wealth. It is very distinct from those that administrate companies in the totalitarian leftist regimes.

The good administrators are those that contribute to the progress of a country. They are those that instead of spending and enjoying the money they earned, preferred to save in order to expand or construct new factories, businesses, or services, and produce more goods, more jobs, and more wealth. However, they are criticized, and even kidnapped and killed as if they cause damage to others. But in contrast, those who earn good salaries in bureaucratic positions are not criticized, though they contribute little to the progress of the country, because they spend everything to find themselves a better life, they are simple consumers. Would this money not be more advantageous if it fell in the hands of entrepreneurial and ambitious people? How would a nation progress if its people and businesses do not progress?

A country is made great with creative and productive work and that is the mission of the businessperson. Just as the mission of a good politician is to maintain the adequate conditions for which everyone works with enthusiasm and generates wealth and well-being. By damaging private businesses, whatever the form, it is not the proprietors that are most damaged, because as the mortals they are, they first will attend to their own needs. The worst damage is done to the country itself and to the neediest, because it is surpluses or profits that are destined to improve salaries or expand or found new business that create more jobs, wealth, and well-being, precisely what makes progress in a country and in the world. Is it so difficult to comprehend that by damaging the producers and proprietors, we are doing worse damage to the country, to those who need work, food, and goods to buy? The worst that a government could do is to take resources from those who produce and create wealth, in order to waste it or make it disappear.

But there are people who prefer to see everyone going through hunger and necessity, before seeing some living better than others. And instead of trying to improve the system in which they enjoy living, they damage it along with their country.

Another thing that is heard is that they want to disinherit their children. Was this not the greatest incentive for their parents? Was it not for them that they worked, so that they didn't have to go through difficult times, and not being taken care of by a third party? And if they disinherit them, they would be taking away the natural right that even animals have, which is protecting their children. In addition, we should keep in mind that the abilities and other qualities also are inherited, the good as well as the bad. And if the parents did good things, it is very probable that their children will as well or even do better than them. Perhaps it is not the children that from a young age learned from their parents about business for this reason are more knowledgeable? Of course yes, not all inherit the good qualities that made their parents triumph. But without a doubt, many did even better than their parents. It also happens that many sell what they inherit. But from the moment that others acquire the property, it will almost always be with the purpose of making it better. Although today they could fall in the hands of figureheads of the left who are enemies of private property, who hoarding capital and monopolize the world economy.

PRIVATE PROPERTY

Is private property an obstacle to making the world more just or more humane?

In what way are profits that companies generate more beneficial for the country, for the workers, and for everyone in general? Could these resources be used better under the administration of the State, or spread among the workers, above all when they want to increase production?

Let us suppose the extreme case that they want the state to take over all the profits of the businesses and the proprietors are left with barely enough to eat; they could increase the tax on the profits to sufficiently high levels to meet this objective, and despite this, the proprietors would continue being proprietors.

Or let us suppose that they want to distribute a large percentage of the profits of the businesses among the workers. They could perfectly approve a law that obligates certain businesses, or all of them, to distribute this percentage, and we would have another direct form of distribution. However, the proprietors would continue being proprietors, which shows that what is needed is not confiscating property, nor is it the case that they want proprietors to make equal or less money than the workers.

But these measures could be very damaging. Because when the profits are shared between the workers, what will probably occur is the economic paralysis of the country. Because by distributing directly the profits of the businesses among the workers, these workers will have more money to buy things, but there will be the same amount of goods or products in the market, so it will provoke an immediate shortage, and the market will not respond to the demand because its owners will not have the resources for it, which will translate into inflation, or into lines and rationing, depending on the measures the government takes. In the end,

113

distributing the profits to the workers would not do anything, because they will have the same amount of goods to purchase.

And if the profits remain in the hands of the government, we all know by diverse experiences of countries that made incursions into leftist totalitarianism, just as they did with national enterprise, that these hands of the state or political party generally do not have to spread around anything. And what are the profits or surpluses that they are set aside for, well for expansion, or for modernization, or for the new businesses that they country needs to grow, or to increase the supply of goods or services, or to increase the workers salaries, or to offer work to the new workers unless the population increase has also been paralyzed. In any case it would not only halt the increase of production and the supply of work, but also modernization would be paralyzed along with the replacement of equipment, just as the creation or placement in practice of new ideas that occur to the proprietor and that could not be realized because he did not have at hand the sufficient resources to execute them. Additionally, we should keep in mind that: by leaving the proprietor without a sufficient share of the profits, he will lose interest, it will not be important to him if the business earns more or less, which will bring as a consequence a lack of stimulus and unproductivity, precisely what had happened with the businesses in the hands of the State or at the hands of the party. For this reason, no matter how good the proprietor or administrator of the company is, in any case, they should have sufficient incentives that translate to a greater material well-being, or other types of privileges that definitively distinguish him from the rest, and situate him in the best economic conditions with respect to the other employees and workers. Because if the destiny of he who administrates is to continue in a condition equal to that of everyone else, obviously, nobody will be interested in taking positions of such great responsibility.

Until now the experience of the whole world has demonstrated that resources or money in the power of the State or a party, as they do not have mourners, it dissolve in the bureaucratic apparatus. Or rather, many people consume and produce little, and this results in the increase in the demand for consumer goods and the stagnation of production, which brings about scarcity and inflation in the countries that have made incursions into the nationalization of business, and to scarcity and rationing in countries where the government controls everything.

In reality the businessman produces for the well-being of all, and the more efficient and productive the business is, the more everyone else benefits from having more to buy and with more accessible prices. And the more profits the business has, the greater the expansion and production capacity they will have, including opening new branches, which translates to a greater supply of work, a greater supply of goods, better wages for the employees and workers, and more substantial payments of the taxes for the maintenance of social security and necessary public works. The fact that the company is growing means that what it produces or trades is being sold, that there is a need for it, and that many people benefit from it. And all this occurs without the intervention of the State.

In addition we all know that the real business people usually improve the living conditions of their employees and workers. For example: Henry Ford on his own initiative and without pressure from anyone doubled the wages of all his employees and workers. Many others followed his example, and many more created foundations and hospitals, and contributed millions of dollars to the well-being of all.

And let us not be so selfish as to look down upon the proprietors that enjoy what they have done, which did not exist before, because they not only receive a well-deserved prize for their hard work, but also at the same time distribute part of the riches that they themselves created to those who

115

are dedicated to other activities. It is also good to remember that after things are made, it is very easy to become accustomed to them, and see them and use them as something that is most normal. And at times we don't even arrive at thinking that we have them and we are able to enjoy thanks to those who with much constancy and tenacity created them. Unfortunately, many do not recognize the merit of their creators, and do not even think of them, or believe that without them everything would have been the same; that those businesses, those goods, or those inventions would have still existed, or that they would continue booming with simple administrators. But that is not the case. Many businesses before their sale or the death of their proprietors deteriorate or disappear. The presence or supervision of their creators or proprietors is very important, because in addition to being those who know the most, they will always be the most invested in improving the businesses. Let us recall the wise refrain: The eye of the owner makes the horse fat.

WHO SHOULD WE COPY?

If what we want is to bring the largest sum of happiness and well-being to all the citizens of a country, what economic and political system and what country should we then copy and take our example? Should it not be from amongst those that have arrived at the highest index of well-being? How then could developing countries progress copying those who after many decades of totalitarian Marxism, and despite the help of the capitalist, never went above mediocrity and still live in large part at the expense of free countries.

Who lives better, the workers and employees of the countries that are currently developed with a system of free enterprise or those that live in countries with totalitarian leftist governments? Then, which system should we copy? What is really what should prevail: submission, inefficiency, unproductivity and low quality of life of the workers and employees of the countries that made incursions into leftist totalitarianism, or liberty, efficiency, productivity and high standard of living of the workers and employees that work in private businesses of the free developed countries? Do we imagine the hardships through which countries with regimes that are enemies of free enterprise still pass, if it were not for the countries with free enterprise from which they obtain loans, goods, foodstuffs, technology and investments of all types? How can there still be people who want a system of government that in all aspects has failed for their country? By God, let us be intelligent. Let us copy what is good. Let us copy the best.

It is unfortunate that there still exist individuals that are influenced by these old and failed theories; that if the class war, that if equality, and if exploitation of man by man. When really the only "achievements" of this ideology have been incalculable damages to humanity, peace, and the progress of the whole world.

117

However, the enemies of free enterprise in their iron-fisted dictatorships maintain in their countries some discipline that free countries could perfectly well copy. For example: severe punishments for the corrupt and for criminals, a zero tolerance for ruckus at universities and high schools, to only admit into public universities the most intelligent, and strict birth control, all of which are easily applied in free countries. But it results that these conducts are not copied. Paradoxically, the first that oppose their implementation in countries with a market system and free enterprise are the enemies of private property. Because when they take power, though it be only partial, the only thing they do is create conflict, dejection, decrease in production, and enormous worsening of the political and economic situation in the world. It is lamentable that many do not realize the real damage that is done by the adversaries of free enterprise. And if they come to deepen this revolution of poverty, scarcity of food and necessary good, will be even more palpable.

But we still have time. We still can copy whatever system we choose. But this is for sure, let us copy what is good, let us always copy the best.

GIVING "WORK" IN ORDER TO GIVE WORK?

For a government, giving "work" is the easiest thing to do. And even more so if the government is dictatorial. For example: it would be enough to make the unemployed open and close doors and then with this activity we would have everyone working. Paying them is also very easy; one only needs sufficient paper and a machine to print bills and so we would have solved the problem of paying everyone.

However, this type of "work" would not serve any purpose, nor would the money that they pay us, if we don't come to get what we want and what we need to buy. It is necessary that the work be productive and efficient so that there are sufficient goods and services, so that they are offered in all moments and can be acquired when they are needed. The jobs should be productive so that what some people produce or help to produce can be exchanged with what the rest produce. If the jobs a government provides do not generate consumer goods, nor do they provide a necessary service, the government will be creating – possibly without wanting to – parasites of the country, or simple consumers (Obama's way).

So then, it is easy to understand that what is important is not having "work," which of course any government could offer at any time, but rather having work that is in some way productive, that contributes to maintaining the supply of goods and services, fills the existing needs and can cover the necessities of all.

By working in something productive, no matter who our employer is, we do the work for ourselves, because, the more we produce, the more we will be able to supply, the more we will have to buy, the more competition there will be, and naturally there will be lower prices.

Just as it is important that the work be productive, it is also important that it be efficient. For example: a village of 500 families, where only the heads of the family work, but who work enthusiastically and efficiently, can produce more goods and services than another village with an equal quantity of families where two members of each family work but whose work is lethargic and inefficient. This means that the first village can live better by exchanging the larger amount of production or by enjoying the goods and services offered, despite the fact that only half of the population works when compared to the second village. The efficiency can be the difference between being a poor country and a rich country. Efficiency is so important, that if in the world only 50% of able people were to work, but they produced with the help of equipment, robots, and computers 100% or more of the foodstuffs, goods, and services that were needed, why would the other 50% need to work? If one day we get to this point, then we could very well impost a tax on 50% of the production and on this we could perfectly sustain the other 50% that do not work, which shows that it is not necessary that all people work. Or we could reduce the work schedule by half so that others had a turn at work. Or we could even implement a policy where everyone has six-month vacations. This means that what is important is not that all work, but rather that sufficient goods and services are produced to cover the needs of all.

Naturally when there are not sufficient goods and services, the worry of the government or of the community should not be giving "work" to everyone, but rather having a sufficient supply, and this cannot be arrived at by placing or maintaining people in unproductive positions, but rather by placing them in areas that increase production.

And when a predatory government takes too much money from its citizens for the services it provides, or with exaggerated taxes, and it does this to sustain an unproductive bureaucracy, or to rob them and finance political projects, it is mistaken and does much damage to its country, because it leaves the citizens without many possibilities of buying, or saving, or for undertaking its projects or ideas that increase production and covers the existing deficit. In the case of Venezuela, with its fabulous petroleum profit, what is correct is to eliminate taxes and finance at the same time those who have good projects, provided we have confidence of the government and the projects of the country. This is so because very few could motivate themselves to work as they should to construct or maintain a business, knowing that it will never belong to them, or at any moment it could be taken away from them. And in the case of other countries, what they should do is reducing taxes so that this money remain at the will of the citizens and other productive entities, (the financial resources that the State wastes) in order to facilitate the increase in production. So people will have a greater power to buy, save or carry out projects that incorporate the productive process. Simultaneously and through which the productive apparatus is expanded, this will absorb the increase in the available workforce which will come as a result of the dismantling of the unproductive bureaucracy. So we convert into producers those who, without having wanted it, lived off of the production of others.

IS NON REMOVABILITY OF WORKERS CONVENIENT?

Another myth is the stability of labor.

Today more than ever it is vital for the survival of countries, like in the former Soviet Union, to restructure their economies. Among other things, they make reforms so that all of the state businesses may be self-sufficient financially, made responsible for their own fiscal health and for bringing about a complete system of accountability for costs and self-financing. What does all this mean? How could they achieve the health of the businesses and make responsible those administrators of each one in order to generate profits or economic benefits and that they can finance themselves? How much freedom will they have to give their directors or managers so that they can pressure or dismiss their employees or workers that do not produce? How much freedom will they have to adjust salaries and the number of workers? How much freedom will they have to adjust the prices of their products in the market? Perhaps the private businesses do not have the same form of managing themselves in free countries? What difference would there be then between them, above all with respect to job security? It would be more than sufficient to convince the most radical of the leftists of the failure of communism as a system and that the only difference between left and right would be, in that with the first (the left way) the businesses would be directed by bureaucrats and with the second (the right way), by their own founders and creators, or inheritors, or later buyers. Which of the two forms is the most efficient and just?

Fortunately politicians and economists understand more and more every day that when the businesses are damaged, be they large or small or private or state-run, the country and the workers are the ones that are most damaged.

However, some still think that non removability is beneficial for the labor sector. But this is not the case, because on making the direction of businesses non removable, they damage the productive apparatus, they damage the whole country in general, and the worst consequences are for the working class.

In all the countries with a market system, almost all of the new businesses start small, with one or two workers, and little by little, some sooner than others, as they prosper, they go about hiring more employees and workers. And some become giant, capable of giving work to thousands of people, of providing services to millions and of producing thousands of tons of foodstuffs and consumer goods. This indicates that the social relations of production have been optimized.

And the more the businesses grow and prosper, the better it will be for the workers and for the whole country in general. On the other hand, when businesses stagnate, employment growth also comes to a halt and the country stops progressing. And if they fail or shut their doors, the country falls behind even more and everyone in general comes out of it having been damaged, because there will be less work and less goods available in the market. But those that suffer most from the bankruptcy of a business are the workers themselves who are left without a job that enables them to obtain the resources they need to live.

There is no boss or private business whose interest is not in prospering. And by progressing, generally they increase the number of workers. For this reasons what is normal for a business that is progressing is not having less, but rather having more workers. Even when they decide to substitute modern machinery for manual labor, that is not done for damaging to the condition of workers, but rather for making the business more efficient, for bettering the factors of production, which causes the business to grow, because what they always end up increasing is the number of employees and workers. For this reason, be the business state-run or private, no matter their size, businesses will see themselves as obligated to reduce personnel for some

123

circumstance, they should not only have the freedom to be able to do it, but rather that they are obligated to do it. And if the government stops them, it damages the business because it cannot balance its costs with the money it has coming in, causing worse damage that could include bankruptcy, which would mean they would have to send to the streets, now not just a few, but rather all of their employees or workers.

It is good to make clear, that the reduction in personnel which the private enterprises see themselves as obligated to impose, is generally motivated by intervention of the state in the economy. These reductions almost always are temporary, while they adjust or normalize the damaging situation created by official interventionism. But always the most interested in rising above these challenges are the owners. But if the State forms an obstacle against the administration of the business, decreeing non removability of labor, the damages could be irreversible. It is indispensible that businesses (large or small, state-run or private) have complete liberty to dismiss or hire at whatever time, whichever workers they consider convenient. Unjustified firings do not exist. When an employer decides to dismiss someone it is because there is a good reason. However unjust the motive may seem, it will never be to damage the business, but rather to benefit it. For example: that there is an antipathy or rivalry between the manager and a worker, that is a sufficient reason to dismiss him or her, because the inconvenience or the problems he has make his work uncomfortable and not completely efficient, which causes damage to the business, just as it does to the workers, the country, and everyone in general.

Another inconvenience of non removability of the labor force, above all when it is permanent, is the propensity of certain workers to not show up, to be lazy, confident in the protection of the non removability status, which translates to inefficiency, higher costs of production and products of worse quality, that will cost all, including the workers themselves, even more when they see the necessity of acquiring them. For all of this, the workers themselves should be the most interested in the business prospering or recuperating, because through its progress they will also progress, the business will be in better conditions to increase salaries and the workers will also be able to make demands. Whatever the motive, one cannot sacrifice all the workers of a business to defend the non removability status of some, and much less if it is circumstantial.

THE DAMAGES OF MONOPOLIES AND PROTECTIONISM

If at this moment the inhabitants of an extraterrestrial world more developed or more sensible than our own, were to observe us, what opinion would they have of us as organized and intelligent beings? It is probable that they would have a very bad concept of us that they would judge us as the most selfish beings in the universe, and that would be the reason that they would kill us or isolate us economically from one another. We are divided into more than 180 countries. Almost all of them strive to be self-sufficient. They try to produce all that they need as if the others were going to cease to exist. All of them want others to buy what they produce but at the same time they do not want to buy what the others are producing. This brings us to protectionism, which brings as a consequence that all countries at an international level come out damaged.

Let us suppose that the world were to be reduced at this moment to just Venezuela, that the other countries did not exist. Suppose that we were complete self sufficient, that among all of the States we could produce all that we use and consume; The State of Zulia is a great producer of petroleum, milk, meat, bananas, etc. and they buy from other states what they produce none or very little of, like cars, spare parts, fabrics, tools, etc that the States of Aragua or Carabobo bring into the Venezuelan economy, states that are characterized by a large level of industrial production. Or like coffee, potatoes, or carrots we the people from Zulia state usually bring in from Andean states. Or cereal grains like rice, sorghum, or corn that we bring in from the States of Portuguesa, Guarico, or Barinas. The Bolivar State is characterized as having great mineral production and a great production of manufactured products like iron and aluminum, which it sells to other states and at the same time it gets from other states the things that it needs but does not produce. And so, all of the regions help one another by providing everything that is necessary. These exchanges, in addition to protecting ourselves by covering the individual needs to each State, also benefits us in price and quality, because just as the Zulians have excellent regions for the cultivation of the banana and it is more economical for us to produce it, in which many factors have an influence like: climactic and topographical conditions as well as cost and efficiency of the labor force, or strategically favorable conditions, like being close to mining sites or other sites that produce raw materials. An aluminum factory that has its source of supply nearby should produce more economical prices than another situated some 1000 kilometers away because of the cost of transport. A sardine packer if it is close to the fishing sites should produce more economically than another that is not so close. In the same way, the consumer will be able to buy the finished products at a better price near the centers of production than in other places where he will have to pay transportation costs. In the same way, a state with a climate and conditions ideal for the production of potatoes, black beans, or wheat will produce more economically than others that may not have those conditions, that those other states will perhaps produce sugarcane or rice more economically if the optimal conditions for these cultivations are reached, and so each region successively have its advantages and disadvantages for producing the infinity of products that go to market, that are indispensible, and that many times are preferable to exchange than to try to produce ourselves. For example: why put so much effort into producing pears and apples if we could just as well exchange them for mangos or other fruits that are easier and more economical for us to produce.

While all the citizens may be free to produce and exchange what they think convenient, without subsidies or protections of any type, the production of the following goods will be stimulated in the region: a) those that do not exist or are in short supply in the market, b) those that can compete in the region or outside of it at more economical prices, c) those that possess a superior quality than those that already exist, and d) those that have at the very least the same price and quality. And this is obvious, because no one would risk producing something that cannot compete with what is already being sold. So healthy competition is formed between producers where the previously mentioned factors come into play, just as the technology, experience, organization, cost of labor, and the motivation of the workers. Where there exists a region that for its conditions does not take part in diversifying or widening its production in a competitive way, there will be a surplus or availability of labor that will emigrate to those states or regions where they are needed.

While the country marches as a whole, without selfishness between the states, everyone benefits from the cheap prices at which domestic products can be sold. Some sell to others what they produce and buy what they need, without duties or prohibitions on the part of state governments, in a free trade environment, at healthy price and quality in a competitive environment. But let's suppose that the governors of one state develop the whim to produce all that they buy from the others because they don't want the money in circulation to escape to other regions. The means of achieving this are: a) subsidize the local producers that have higher costs so that they can sell at the same prices or better prices as the foreign producers; this means artificial prices and a fiscal burden for the contributors that will become unbearable as time passes and will traumatize the consumer b) to prohibit buying less necessary things or limiting external purchases; this will cause a deterioration in the quality of life of those who buy, and scarcity and price increases not only of what they stop importing, but also of all the products related to those imported products, and also will cause a recession in the states that produce it. And finally, the most common: to apply high taxes to the articles that come from far away in order to protect the local producers and the crops that they want to develop; this also will automatically provoke scarcity, make prices rise for the consumer, and will lower the quality of many products that will not have outside competition. When a state begins protectionism in order to make itself self-sufficient, others who see themselves damaged will imitate them: Zulia will apply high taxes to vehicles and to the other things that it brings in from far away so that there is local incentive to produce and avoid the drain of currency; in the state of Bolivar as a consequence, the industrial states could apply high taxes to gas and to the agricultural products that are brought from afar, seeking to incentivize local production. With the increased price of gas, the cost of transport will increase and all will be affected, vehicles will go up in price, agricultural and industrial machinery, parts and electrical artifacts, farmers will see themselves as obligated to increase the prices of the products and with this the byproducts and derivatives, and it is possible that even some farmers that were modernizing would go back to oxen and horses because of the impossibility of acquiring the expensive equipment and the gas. And so each state successively will try to protect what belongs to it, applying protectionist measures that damage everyone. If to this, we add the monopolization of production in order to increase prices of products like petroleum, in the style of OPEC, the situation will get worse at the regional level, just like those occasional damages that this monopoly will cause at a worldwide level.

What is incredible is that this is actually occurring now, the difference is in scale, that instead of being at the level of States or regions, it is occurring at the level of countries, even more serious because of its reach, which puts the world in crisis. And it would not be strange that later, following the selfishness and protectionism between countries, that it would be extended to the level of states or municipalities, to fall even lower in this historic recession, in which all of humanity instead of benefitting from the abundance and from the low prices that are generated by free competition, efficiency and technology, is damaged by protectionism and by the monopolies that bring about inefficiency, backwardness, scarcity, and inflation. We now feel the crisis and the unemployment at a world level as a consequence of the artificial increase of the price of petroleum. Fortunately the food producers have not created monopolies to increase the prices as the petroleum exporters did in order to multiply the price sometimes even by 20. The ideal, correct, and logical way is to see the world as a whole, as the brothers that we are; that each country, state or person has complete freedom to produce what he can or wants to, without protectionisms or monopolies of any type, so that we can introduce products into the local or international market in a competitive fashion and everyone can benefit from the abundance, quality, and low prices that efficiency and free competition generate.

SPECULATION OR EXAGERATED PRICES

This is another of the absurd beliefs because of which some functionaries think they should intervene. That with the exception of them, the other people are stupid or silly, and as if we were babies, they have to protect us.

Who can speculate about the price of products in the United States? Perhaps this occurs because the North American government prohibits things from being sold above certain prices? Just the opposite. In the United States no one can speculate with the price of produces because the government does not intrude in these things (except recently in the Obama's way).

In a free market, the speculator falls by his own weight because everyone is free to "speculate." For example: if you think that onions are too expensive and that onions make the best business in the world, why do you not take advantage of the situation and make yourself a millionaire by dedicating yourself to selling onions? Ah! It is not the vendors who speculate, but rather the transportation workers, well then why do you not take advantage of the situation and make yourself a transport worker? Ah! It is not the transport workers, but rather the planters, then why do you do take advantage of earning more and start to plant and harvest onions? And if you do not want to do any of this, you are still free to buy or not buy onions, but please, do not think that they are speculating with the price. And this is what really occurs in a free market; the people are encouraged to sell, make, plant, or import something when they see that it is a good business. And this is precisely what stops scarcity, lack of competition, hoarding, and high prices.

Although it seems contradictory, the only way of speculating with the price of a product is in a market that someone has intervened in. Because the regulations bring scarcity and this is the principal cause of price increases and they can speculate with a product.

131

Let us view the facts: If a government regulates the selling price of the tomato, and the farmers conclude that it is no longer a good business, the most probable thing is that they will not grow them anymore, or they will grow very few. The result will be a scarce harvest of tomatoes. The supply will be poor, less than the demand, and this will make it so that many people will not be able to buy tomatoes. And those who need to buy them surely will have to pay a higher price (black market) or rather, that the same consumer will be responsible for offering more and increase the price of the product. This is what happens normally when a product becomes scarce, unless the leftist totalitarian regime model is adopted: the model of lines and rationing. However, the producers do not benefit from the high prices of the black market, they would not have an incentive and the problem of scarcity and high prices would persist. On the other hand, when the prices are kept free and scarcity pushes them up, then the farmers do benefit from it, they receive the incentive of the better prices, they plant more, and in turn they attract new planters. As a result, there will be a large harvest that automatically will make prices decrease, because you cannot speculate with something that exists in abundance, and even less if the produce is perishable and costly to store. The farmers, shopkeepers, and growers know this and it can be observed at any moment. The same happens when a government regulates prices of industrial production; the difference is that it takes more time for the scarcity to present itself. Then, as the costly infrastructure and machinery is already in place, they will meanwhile try to get some benefit out of it. But no one will get excited about investing in other factories or industries that do not generate the sufficient and necessary capital gains for their own maintenance, replacement of equipment and adequate profits. In contrast, when no regulations exist, they can see the higher prices, so it then becomes a good business that will attract new investors that will construct new industries and will have to compete against themselves, which will result in a better quality and lower prices.

But it is good to make clear that those who are most interested in selling what they produce or trade are the makers and shopkeepers themselves, and for this it is indispensible that the products please the people and that they like the price. For this reasons it is the same producers and shopkeepers that should determine the price on their own goods without anybody's interference.

If Marx and Engels were not mistaken in something, it was their description in an eloquent form of the creative and productive capacity of private business. And referring to its grand expansion they observed: "Low prices of their goods are the heavy artillery that topples all of the Great Walls of China and the most fanatically barbarian person, hostile to foreigners, capitulate." As an example we can mention the great success and progress of the Japanese and of other Asian countries where governments never intervened to regulate their products.

Marx and Engels, the same men that forecasted the self-destruction of capitalism due to the epidemic of super production, would have their mouths dropped open today on seeing some countries suffering from scarcity and inflation, because their leftist governors believe in speculation, they regulate the prices and create an obstacle to production.

A market of free prices has always been the natural thing, and it is inseparable from the freedom of business, from free initiative, and from the respect for private property. The regulations of these liberties come out of countries that made incursions into leftist totalitarianism and in others with the same type of governors. The regulations produce scarcity and this drives the rationing that is incompatible with the free world.

All industry or commerce needs to sell its products, and if it does not sell or sells very little, it fails. It is an economic law that when prices increase, sales decrease, and this has never been nor will be the way a business prospers.

For this reason, in a natural market, without intervention, the interest of the business owner is to increase sales, not to increase prices.

A few years ago, in Venezuela price regulations and controls did not exist. There was not speculation and the markets were packed with food and goods of all types at low cost. But when the leftists came to power, they started the controls and regulations that brought as a consequence the scarcity, disappearance, or price increase of many products. After some years, they freed the prices, and to top it off, at the same time, they took away the subsidies on many products. Naturally, abrupt increases were produced. The leftists took advantage of this to blame others and make the freeing of prices an unpopular measure. One of its arguments against it was that the conditions for freeing the prices were not given because of a lack of competition, when it is precisely the controls and regulations that are an obstacle and that end with competition.

All developed countries in the world went through the stage of the first factory or industry of a product and in none of them was it necessary to regulate prices because there was not competition. Competition did not appear by magic. Competition was made, and for competition to occur there must be a freedom of prices.

And there are so many things that can have a bearing on the costs of a product: administrative and labor efficiency, locality and situation, the cost of raw materials, transport, distribution, insurance, travel allowances, etc., that for those who are in charge of regulating products, there is no alternative other than placing a maximum price for public sale, leaving a sufficient margin for those that have higher costs, or for those who are more inefficient. But those who could very well sell at a lower price (because they have a lower cost of production) take advantage of this. So the one who comes out damaged from this is the consumer. The same occurs at the level of the distributor or retailer, because of differences in location, costs of transport, rent, or more luxurious locales and furnishings. At the end of the day, because of regulations, the consumer pays the consequences.

Another harmful factor that has a bearing on regulated prices is the great responsibility and wisdom of those who have the delicate and complicated task of fixing prices on the infinity of models and qualities of a product (shoes for example). How many mistakes could there be, or how many deals could they make with the manufacturers?

In a free market, the public is the best judge. The public decides if the product is worth buying, if it stops buying the product or finds a substitute in another product. And when the public doesn't like the price, it can visit other stores and buy where it is more convenient. And if the brand is bad quality, it is certain that the consumer will not buy it again. This is one of the other reasons for which we should combat the falsification of brands because with these falsifications the public is deceived and the manufacturers are damaged. In whichever case, he who abuses the client, be it the merchant or the manufacturer, he will face the consequences, because it will be difficult for the consumer to stick with the product, having been tricked, unless there are not other alternatives because of a lack of competition, which is very rare in a market free of regulation.

Regulations more than other government interventions, can be responsible for the bankruptcy or stagnation of many businesses, and of making the proprietors lose confidence and enthusiasm, who then become: some, simple speculators, and others complainers who beg the government for higher prices as the simplest and quickest form of obtaining profitability, with the consequence of loss of efficiency and low production. And the most important: the lack of stimulus to create new industries and trades, or to widen the existing one for a greater production and competition that drives progress and development.

And without a doubt, the regulations drive scarcity, and scarcity drives price increases. In contrast, when the government does not intrude, every person is the true master of what he or she does, buys, sells, plants, invents, inherits, or is given as a gift. In other words, when people are free to price things on their own, then supply and demand function in their natural way, and production and prices balance each other by the natural and universal law.

In a free market it is the manufacturers or merchants who worry most about offering the best prices in order to get new clients, or the keep their clients.

With this regulation of the prices of products, governments make idiots of the people. Fortunately, there are merchants, and even in these circumstances, almost all the articles they sell with prices that are below regulations; certainly, it is these businesses that sell more and for this reason they are the most prosperous. This shows us that the regulations only serve to increase the prices to the consumer.

Do you think that because regulations do not exist, merchants could fix their prices very high in order to earn more? If someone does that, it is certain that in a very short time he should close or sell his business, because it is the very merchants or manufacturers who should worry about keeping a price that the public agrees with, on the contrary, they fail, unless they are very luxurious and selective businesses that are only accessible to people with a lot of buying power who prefer to pay more in exchange for luxury, convenience, and personalized service.

It is the governments with their power and their preferences that create monopolies and hoarding, because it is through them that import licenses are given, permission for businesses and even preferential spending. The same happens with the distribution of what the inefficient state businesses produce.

Another of the motivations for which regulations make everything more expensive is because there are so many articles produced and so many differences that exist in the costs of production between one factory and another, or from one business to another, that it is very difficult to define costs. For this reason the functionaries have no other alternative than to accommodate the prices according to the costs and the complaints of the most inefficient that are protected from bankruptcy by the selling prices.

By contrast, in a market free from regulations, each one defends himself as he can. The inefficient ones see themselves as obligated to compete with the most efficient, as much in price as in quality. They either correct themselves or adapt to the market, or they disappear. This translates to a greater worry on the part of the producers to lower their costs, increasing the quality and improving their products.

The only way a business continues speculating or tricking people is while it is protected or monopolized by the State.

Unfortunately, there are still those who put forth the effort to blame producers and merchants. And this is not true. The only way to speculate for an indefinite time is while regulations or price impositions are imposed by the government, because these serve as a pretext or as support for the inefficient merchants and as trickery and confusion to the consumer. They are also to blame that some businesses close or stop producing some things, because, whether for ignorance, or for electoral or populist causes, after increasing the salaries or devaluing the currency, they were not permitted to increase the prices of products. This causes shortages, and shortages cause inflation, creating a vicious circle made worse in a short time by paralyzing the provided expansions and the projects of the new businesses that would come to produce, compete, and fill a need in the market. Economic liberty, by governing the demand of the supply of the market, puts an end to all these irregularities, because the

137

whole market is free to put a price to its things, generating competition, abundance and low prices. At the same time the officials working in "consumer protections" jobs are eliminated, which will see themselves as obligated to work in something generating production and to contribute to supply. So the constant bribery of merchants and manufacturers to these "consumer protections" bureaucrats will cease, which at the same time would mean lower costs of production and lower prices for the consumer.

ARE MANDATORY SALARY INCREASES BENEFICIAL?

At first glance these mandatory salary increases, such as that of minimum wage, seem like something just, however mandatory salary increases are damaging.

Mandatory salary increases are like a boomerang that returns but leaves everyone, above all workers, in worse economic conditions than those before the increases. Many countries have experienced this, and in all of them, the employees and workers reduced the buying power of the increases later. For this reason, it is strange that someone would still insist on mandatory increases, unless he really wants bad things for the poor, who are definitely the most damaged by this process.

Because when a government obligates the whole economy of a country to increase the wage for the workers, a series of negative phenomena are produced that damage the whole world and that fact we will attempt to expose in this chapter.

Very few people will not agree that the employees and workers who make more money spend more. But the general mandatory increase, just like minimum wages, damages the workers and everyone in general, because the only thing they do is to earn more in order to later buy less than what they bought before the increases.

And it has nothing to do with the fact that the problem is speculative as a large part of the population is made to believe. If this were the reason, the workers and employees in totalitarian countries in the hands of the left would live like kings, because the government and the party, being owners of the means of production, could very well decree the very greatest salary increases for everyone, maintaining product prices. However, they do not do this, for the simple reason that they would have more money to buy, but the quantity of goods and services would remain the same. The only thing they could do is increase the waiting lists and the rations, which are not most extreme thanks to the generosity of capitalist countries from which these countries obtain food, technology, and funds.

The main problem consists of the fact that it is very easy to make decrees and make people comply with the increase of salaries but it is impossible to decree and make people comply with the increase in production. This means that in reality the only thing that they accomplish with mandatory increases is to distribute more money amongst the same amount of goods. If things stayed that way it would not be such a serious matter, but another series of negative phenomena occur to make the situation worse. First because the more needy people in any country are the unemployed and the governments are obligated to incentivize productive employment so that these most needy are helped, but upon decreeing new minimum wages, they succeed in doing the opposite, or increasing the number of unemployed. To top off all of these bad things, it will be much more difficult for the most needy to survive because of the increased prices that came as a consequence of the mandatory increases.

And it is not that the damage occurs to a small minority while the rest benefit from it; the cruel reality is that in a short time everyone will have come out of it having been damaged.

Another phenomenon that occurs with the new minimum wages is that the workers that earn the same or more than that salary which is fixed by the decree, observe how other people without the least effort come to earn the same as them, and they also realize, that if they did not increase their salary, they will come out of this very affected by not being able to acquire, with the same money, what they used to buy before the increases. This morally obligates the bosses to increase the salary of all the others as well, in order to avoid this deterioration, and at the same time to maintain the difference in salary for those who deserve it. This is almost equivalent to a general increase in wages and salaries that is one of the principal causes of inflation, because it increases the cost of manual labor and of all the materials that are being produced. However, there will be many businesses, above all the medium and small ones, that cannot increase the salary of everyone, which will be tremendously negative for the workers and employees that stay at their same salary level, and that will have to pay more for everything as a consequence of the mandatory increases.

In contrast, when minimum wages do not exist, or rather in normal conditions of the free market, any person could be employed at convenience between the parts and according to the possibilities and needs of each part. With this, two very important things are achieved: one of which is to give work to him who needs it, who still earning less than the rest, prefers this to not earning anything; and the other is, that these new employees that were a burden on society before, begin to produce, which brings with it an increase in the supply of goods and services.

Another inconvenience that occurs with mandatory increases is that a great part of small businesses see the need to work as a family: wife, children, etc... as a form of not being affected by the increases in minimum wages and the consequent increase of social assistance (where it exists). But this form of operation is limiting, and because of this causes stagnation or detriment to the economy. We should keep in mind that the current large companies were small in their beginnings. Because of this if small businesses are not permitted to grow, we automatically do away with the future large companies.

Another problem that everyone is now familiar with is that many people see the necessity of going to informal work, with the consequent proliferation of peddlers and street vendors.

141

In addition, when minimum wages to not exist, whichever person could be employed by another without worrying about having low performance, or that does not have experience in the work; this is compensated with the pay that the boss and the worker agree upon, and with the condition that his production increases along with his experience, so that his salary will become equal with the rest of the employees. This at the same time is a stimulus for the worker who will try to produce equal amount or more than the others and doing things better in order to try to excel and get a better salary. In contrast, by obliging the payment of a minimum wage to those who can not make the same amount labor or work as the rest, they will not be given work, or they will be fired immediately, many times without realizing the cause of their dismissal. Also for this reason the elderly and young people without experience will be marginalized.

How many times has it happened to you, that you see someone in need, and wanted to employ him and pay him according to his availability, and despite all that, you refused, because they make you pay a minimum wage with their respective social benefits? How many businesses or companies close before they even open their doors because the future businessman does not have sufficient funds to pay the minimum salary?

Another negative aspect of mandatory salary increases and the obligatory social benefits is that the workers also are damaged in terms of stability of their work, because, as a way of avoiding government impositions, bosses try, in terms of what is possible, to convert permanent positions into seasonal positions.

Another problem derived from mandatory increases is that the quality of some products goes down, because sufficient stimulus does not exist in the worker to improve the quality of his work, or at the very least to maintain it with the purpose of improving his salary, simply because it is the State that takes the principal role in improving the salary of everyone, so the employees may not be doing things as they should.

The mandatory increases are equally damaging because they increase the bureaucratic costs that are not productive. It diverts funds that could be used to improve health, education, or security, or for financing the productive equipment. It also discourages investors, the foreign as much as the national.

On the other hand, in countries with a free market economy and free enterprise, it is a common practice of any employer to periodically increase the pay of employees and workers to provide them with an incentive or stimulus, to reward and try to improve their productivity, which everyone benefits from. But when the state takes for itself this practice that doesn't belong to it, the tendency of the employers is to not increase the pay of the workers in order to avoid a double increase, or a larger one if this is done based on the percentage of what the worker earns at the present time.

On the other hand there are businesses that have higher costs of production and sell at the highest prices. And by being obligated to increase their salaries, in addition to increases in the raw materials and the services that come after the increases, they would have to sell to the public at even more inaccessible prices, which would cause many businesses to close, with the known negative consequences which are: more workers in the streets, and more falling behind and more in poverty. Others would look for a way to operate with fewer workers in order to be able to subsist, by which they also damage the workers in terms of the stability of their employment, because some could be let go because the bosses were trying to balance things out or avoid bankruptcy, which would also be very negative for everyone, although not to the same degree as if the were obligated to keep the same number of workers.

The compulsive increases in salary also can stand in the way of exportation because they increase the cost of production. They also bring about damages and setbacks because of the uncertainty and the fear of the news stories or journalistic speculation about possible new increases.

Another way in which it decreases production is because each productive entity – be it a business, industry, or commerce – is in different conditions with respect to others. And it is illogical to think that a government can solve all of them and each one of these aspects in order to later adapt a decree for each one. To mention some problems, in many cases they would be forcing the producer to spread around the money destined for investment, and in other cases the producer will see himself as obligated to fire workers in order to confront the new increases. But the most damaging is the discouragement that spreads among the producers and investors, conscious of the damage they are doing to the country and to everyone in general.

The mandatory salary increases cause damage, because whatever type of economic policy they come to implement, the first ingredient to production is the workforce. It is the only thing that is present in all production activities. Naturally, in a market economy it is the first thing that should be submitted to supply and demand.

By leaving the workforce free, the workforce acquires its just value: people who are diligent, willing, responsible, or more capable will be the most sought after and the best paid; by contrast the lazy and irresponsible will see themselves as obligated to change if they want to keep their jobs or be better paid. In the same way, people who are more qualified or that worry about learning, also will be more sought after and better paid.

To earn more in order to buy less is to do a tremendous wrong to all the workers and at the same time to the country in general. What the whole world wants is to be able to buy more with what they earn in the moment. But this is only achieved by governments that leave those who work and produce in peace, so that every one in his own field can achieve efficiency and productivity, the only way of making things cheaper and being able to offer them at a lower price. By taking away all of these obstructions, spontaneous increases in salary will automatically reappear, which is normal in authentic free market economies even in conditions of deflation.

It is very important that the businesses as much as the workers have the freedom to agree upon the conditions of work without any type of interference. The increases should be made by the bosses so that there is a stimulus to increase production and to improve the quality of what is produced, which at the same time will permit competition in national and international markets. Labor freedom is another difference between those countries that prosper and those that go backwards or stagnate.

Any country that respects private property and lets the market fix the guidelines progresses rapidly. This was precisely what happened in Japan and in other Asian countries, and now also in China which has more of an economic workforce, diligent and disciplined, this incentivizes work as well as investments of capital. The progress it generates can come to employ the entire available workforce, and reverse the situation: The workers become expensive, scarce, and sought after, they have many offers for work, and they put themselves in positions of demand. They move on to better socioeconomic conditions. This occurred in all countries that developed with free market economies and it still occurs in politically stable countries, with a diligent economic workforce, where they permit the free market to function, and impositions to hire or fire workers do not exist.

Mandatory salary increases that impoverish are one thing, and spontaneous increases that employees deserve are a very different thing, that generally comes along with the prosperity of the business.

When governments dedicate themselves only to what they should do and to what they are elected, which is guaranteeing order and protecting and respecting all the citizens and their property, prosperity comes on its own, as has been demonstrated in many countries. In contrast when a government intervenes, even if it trying to make things better, and it imposes mandatory salary increases, it immediately affects the production process and damages the entire country, above all the employees and workers who depend on the prosperity and development of businesses, be they large or small.

Mandatory increases in the end are made to spread more money over the same amount of products or services, or even fewer goods than what there previously were before the mandatory increase. These mandatory increases that are one of the principal motivations of those who have spent a few months in power however have made things worse for the whole world. On top of that, they will have lost valuable time that would have resulted in more suffering for the poor and for the unemployed that definitively are the most damaged. To avoid all of these negative aspects, employers should have the security that there will not be mandatory increases, and for this reason it is important that free market economies are protected under the law against this type of interventionism. Without a doubt there will be more stimuli to work and to produce things even more efficiently.

PAYING THE LEAST POSSIBLE AMOUNT TO THE WORKER?

The Marxists signal that the private capitalists will try to pay the least amount possible to the workers in order to obtain more profits. Would it not be the opposite? Who earns more and lives better: the current workers in state businesses in Russia or China, or the workers of private businesses in the United States, Canada, or Western Europe? In Russia and China there currently exist both types of businesses: those that still continue to be in the hands of the regime, and the private businesses of foreign investors. And in which do the workers earn more?

Because all good bosses know that in order to prosper and be efficient, the worker should be happy, should be pleased, excited, given incentives, and be well paid in accordance with the possibilities of the business. Unhappy workers are unproductive; they do not perform, work with a bad attitude and damage the business. For this reason, the interest of the intelligent owner will always be to give the worker an incentive, to have him in the best possible, most enthusiastic state; if not he fails as an owner and as a businessman, and other people will sell and will have to make the product better, or the pattern will repeat itself. Few cases are known where the employees and workers do not better their standard of living while their business prospered.

As a general rule, when a business prospers, its employees and workers also prosper. When a business progresses, it is good for its owners, it is good for its employees and workers, it is good for the country, and it is good for the consumers who also benefit from it.

We should be conscious that the owner or proprietor is a simple administrator of the goods that in practice are everyone's. So much so that he can die and the business continue to benefit the country and its citizens.

147

Certainly, there are thoughtless owners, although they are rare, because obviously they all fail in business. But, perhaps by passing the businesses into the hands of the State the workers will be managed by a better boss? Generally the most despotic bosses exist in these regimes, be it because of party support, or because they are incompetent, or because the workers are made to endure it in silence, so it's the same manager on all sides, that dictates the conditions that everyone has to agree to. On the contrary, in a free market and free enterprise system, these abuses are self-correcting because the workers are free to look for a better boss or a better job and they do not have to put up with being walked all over by anyone. In addition, because of the economic growth in these countries and the scarcity of a workforce, the workers are more appreciated and better paid, as has occurred in effect in Japan, Taiwan, and in many other developed countries. And if this did not occur, it was because of the large supply of a workforce that comes from other countries looking for a better life, or from refugees who flee tyrannical regimes who arrive seeking freedom and work at whatever price and compete with current workers and employees. This is the case in the United States and Spain.

It is be very difficult to find a boss who has intentionally diminished the salaries of the workers in order to obtain more profit. And if anyone were to do it, he would probably be without workers, provided that this country is not passing through a great crisis in which workers took joint initiative to reduce their salaries to save the business that was passing through difficulties and they preferred to earn less rather than lose their jobs.

Unfortunately in some countries, the salaries of the employees and the workers are not determined by supply and demand, but rather by the interventions of the State which distorts and impoverishes.

BUSINESSMEN: SHOULD THEY MAKE THE SAME AS EVERYONE ELSE?

Let's talk about how businesspeople and business administrators, without doing harm to anybody and helping even more people, gain the right to earn more than other employees and workers.

Let's take a State business and compare it to a similar one in terms of capital and number of people who work there, but that is administered or supervised by its owner. Let's suppose that the two produce furniture. How many sets are produced in each one? We could come up short on the numbers, because it is not surprising to anyone that a business administered or supervised by its own owner is more efficient than another administered by the State because of the reasons previously mentioned in "Surplus Value," because of the ideas they are putting into practice through the years to achieve a greater production and profitability. Now let us suppose that the business administered or supervised by its owner, produces 30 sets of furniture more per month than its counterpart run by the State with the same costs. Cannot the owner have the right to display those extra 30 sets he produced, sell them and use the money for private expenses? Without damaging anyone and benefiting even more people, he sells them and buys what he desires if the other businesses also produce a higher quantity of goods and services than those than they would have produced if they had been administered by the State. Upon producing all of these efficiently, they all gain the right to exchange something of what they produced in excess in order to use the profits to their own benefit. We ask the question in this way to make it more understandable. What is normal is that with one part of the money of the sales of what was produced in excess, they buy what they want.

And how many more would not be produced by all of the businesses run by the State than if they were privately functioning all the time? Probably the business would be

149

converted into a true giant, benefitting even more people and paying its workers better, as we know happens in large private businesses.

IS LUXURY INSANE?

Many tend to criticize those who buy luxury cars, or large houses, or art paintings or very expensive decorations. But that doesn't hurt anyone. Really what rich people are doing is good, because by spending money on things, they benefit many others who also need to live and eat. For example: in just one of their houses they employ a carpenter, electrician, engineer, architect, bricklayer, plumber, worker and an infinity of other people who take part in the making of all the materials that are used in the construction. Similarly, when they buy a luxurious car, they give work to those who were a part of its making, and to those who directly or indirectly supplied materials or pieces for its construction. And if they buy a beautiful piece of jewelry, a fine adornment, or a good painting, they will give work to all those artists who will be economically repaid according to the quality of their work. Or perhaps artists do not also have the right to live and to eat? And if the private individuals cannot buy the artwork, who then would buy them? Perhaps the State would be under the obligation to buy the hundreds of millions of works of art that painters, sculptors and artists can produce? Would they not spend more maintaining the bureaucracy that would need to catalogue these works and decide even perhaps in an incorrect and unjust way, what paintings are worth the paid they buy, which ones they should eliminate, and which deserve prizes? And who would receive these works of art? Perhaps they would be sponsored by the people with the most influence and power? This is in contrast to a free market, where everything has its just value, because the whole world is free to qualify, reject, offer and buy, without the biased influence of those who control all the media.

In the same way, when we criticize a millionaire because he has spent a scandalous sum of money in a party, we judge him poorly. When we say that he has wasted money when there are so many needy people, we are judging him wrongly. Perhaps by having the party, he is distributing

151

money and performing a social duty? Or perhaps all the people who work and make things for this great party do not have the right to eat? From the farmer who plants the flowers, the deliveryman who bring them, the artists that arrange the flowers, those that rent the chairs and tables, the cooks that prepare the food, the waiters, the workers and employees of liquor, soda, and ice factories, those from the hotel where they rent the ballroom, the photographers, the decorators, the musicians, etc. Everyone has the right to live and to eat. And to prohibit them from giving these grand parties would be to damage the millions of people that participate in creating them and to obligate them to make their living in another way by preventing to them from exercising their profession. In reality, he who holds the party gives work to others. What is important is that there exist enough consumer goods so that every citizen can get them when they need them. There is not sin where they do not let food or goods go to waste. Really people who go to a party change the site of their meal, that's all. Instead of eating in their house, this time they will do it in a ballroom at a hotel or club. And no one should prohibit them from eating outside of their home sometimes, just as on certain occasions they eat less, more, or simply do not eat.

Everyone has the sacred right to live in the way that pleases him as long has he does no damage to others. From those who dedicate themselves to making articles of luxury, to the artists who make jewelry out of gold and precious stones, or those who make decorations out of ceramics or crystal, or those who risk their lives looking for lost treasures at the bottom of the sea, or those artists who are capable of making such exceptional painting that only a government or the most rich could buy it. But all of these people together in a free country could not equal the power that the high functionaries have in a totalitarian Marxist country, with the great difference being that in a free country all people with the ability and sufficient will can get some power by their own merit, or by way of overcoming obstacles, having creativity and constancy and without having to confine themselves to the decisions of bureaucrats, while in those totalitarian countries, power is monopolized and eternalized, and possibly in people without the capacity or the merit for it.

CONTROL OF THE BIRTH RATE

Frequently we observe moving reports in the media that are done in places of extreme poverty. The spectacle is depressing: miserable dwellings and shortages that the mothers who are interviewed relate while surrounded by their raggedy group of malnourished kids.

It is a shame to see these most needy trying to support so many numerous children, despite the fact that they did not want to have so many kids. It is difficult for them to avoid pregnancies because of their lack of knowledge or resources. And they even ignore many different methods of avoiding pregnancy. How many families are needy because of having so many children? Or perhaps it is those who are most poor who generally tend to have the larger families? Would things not be very different if instead of eight it was two children that they had to feed, clothe, and educate?

How can they abandon the poorest to having all of the children in the world, so that there are later more people to directly or indirectly feed, cure, dress, and educate? This marginal world is the human flesh from were these reports are nurtured, reports done by those who seem to want to do everything they can for the poor. It is hypocrisy at its maximum expression: on one side they are abandoned to the macabre destiny of bringing children into the world by the dozens in order to be hungry and in need, in order to later exploit this situation for their ideology. They nourish themselves on this as a vampire nurtures itself on blood to survive.

Does the media in free countries worry about helping to solve these serious problems from which we derive so many other problems? Do the leaders of the different churches worry about orienting their parishioners toward the obsolete regulation of the Catholic Church which only permits the rhythm method of avoiding pregnancy? Is it such a serious sin to use some other contraceptive method?

Perhaps a couple should only have intimate relations in order to have children? If it was so, it would be sinful to have relations with one's wife if she is pregnant, or when she is not fertile, or after menopause. With the ability that God gives us to discern and differentiate the good from the bad, we believe that it is a worse sin to let millions of children be brought into the world to starve and be in need. It is time that the Church adopts a more modern viewpoint in this area, and the church is all of us.

The distribution of children is not a problem, nor is wealth. Nothing is gained by taking away from some in order to give to others. The problem is abandonment, and the solution is to create awareness, to orient and help those who need it. And it is not so difficult to achieve, nor is it so costly that we shouldn't be able to finance it. To confront this problem is very simple if we compare it with that of resolving the most severe and complicated problems caused by it.

Birth control in a society is so indispensible, so civilized, so human, and so intelligent, as using a vaccine to prevent a disease. Just as there exists an abysmal difference between the cost of a vaccine and the cost of a disease, equal or greater difference exists between voluntary family planning, in terms of what it means for society, and the high costs of feeding, clothing, keeping healthy, and educating those children whose parents didn't want them because they did not have the time nor the resources to raise them. Upon becoming adults it is difficult for them to get a job because there was not an adequate relationship between the increase in population and economic growth.

Neither does it have to do with abandoning the children that currently need help. This could be like denying a cure to a sick person because unfortunately they were not vaccinated. But an intelligent and civilized society cannot continue acting in a primitive and irresponsible way. It prefers to confront death, suffering, or the high costs of

155

curing the disease, to intelligent and economical prevention by vaccine, like family planning according to the will and the possibilities of the couple. Neither does it have to do with being in favor of abortion. Nor going to such extremes as in China, where penalties exist and women are forced into abortions. We cannot sympathize more with these people for how inhumane those methods are that can only be done in regimes where fanaticism and ideology are placed above people's lives. It has to do with preventing undesired pregnancies in the same way that campaigns are waged to prevent diseases. It has to do with changing the macabre destiny of bringing children into the world that will live through calamities. It has to do with avoiding the serious problems that originate in society. It has to do with reverting to the situation in developing countries. So there are no more unemployed workers so that the demand will not be more than the supply. Thus the workers would remain at an advantage in front of the employers who will be obliged to pay the highest salaries to the workforce they need, above all in free countries where everyone has complete freedom, so much freedom that they can choose the work that is most pleasing to them.

But it is important that the leaders of all countries in the world know and understand that the large part of new births are produced in overpopulated nations of the Third World, or rather in those countries that find the most difficulty today in providing food, water, work, and sanitation to their inhabitants. That overpopulation is a cause of ruin and is not beneficial and the accelerated growth of the population constitutes a slowing of economic development.

TYPES OF DICTATORSHIPS

The act of mentioning progress that happens in some dictatorships does not mean that we are in favor of them. We believe that democracy is the best form of government. But we can still learn from the experience of dictatorships.

Some people generalize when referring to dictatorships, as if all were the same. Others, because of their political beliefs, neglect to criticize the most tyrannical. We will try to examine them in objectively and in great detail, noting their pronounced differences, as much in economic terms as in terms of freedoms of its citizens. We will also analyze those dictatorships that generate the most progress and well-being.

We can divide them into four categories: 1.- the fierce enemies of free enterprise, where everything is controlled by and is the property of the party, like that of Cuba. 2.- The anticommunist military dictatorships that support private business and the free market like that of Pinochet in Chile. 3.- The military dictatorships of the left, which are interventionist, nationalist, and have a phobia of the United States (like Chavez). 4.- And lastly those of the left that permit private business like that of China. And it is not too strange the idea that this last one could be the future government of the planet, not because it is the best, but rather because of the manipulation of information, both economic and political.

The most significant dictatorships, as much for their military prowess as for their global expansionism, were given the name "dictatorships of the proletariat." It was the only way of imposing these regimes that were by their nature so radical, characterized by the fact that they were founded in the name of the people. They were characterized as "dictatorships of the proletariat" probably so that the people would tolerate the great human sacrifice that was imposed upon them, while they waited for a supposed well-being that

157

never arrived. In effect, after many decades of terror and the largest human sacrifice that any people have ever had to go through, the well-being never came, and that equality that was so extolled really existed, but it was an equality of poverty, backwardness, scarcity, sadness, and desperation. This persisted until they decided to change, and forget the failed Marxist theories, and they opened their doors to private initiative and foreign capital, and lifted the price controls and introduced incentives for productivity just like the capitalists. Today Continental China progresses in an accelerated manner, though it continues to be a dictatorship.

On the other hand we have anticommunist military dictatorships, which respect private business, are conservative in their politics of economic liberty and let the free market function on its own. We do not know of one that currently exists. And like that of China, there is much more economic and social progress observed in anticommunist dictatorships –which the media never seems to see as important-- like that of Franco in Spain, Pérez Jiménez in Venezuela, or that of Augusto Pinochet in Chile, which after economic strangulation caused by some years of a procommunist regime, experienced the greatest economic growth of any of the principal nations of America when they liberated the economy of state control. Milton Friedman, winner of the Nobel prize in economics, and teacher of many of the economists that Pinochet assigned to the reconstruction of the country, signaled that "the true Chilean miracle is not that the free market system has produced a result, but rather that their military government has permitted it to function." These dictatorships, almost always of short duration, give more freedoms than many others. Those that complain the most about these types of dictatorships are the communists and other enemies of private property.

In terms of freedoms that are permitted to its citizens, there is a large difference between dictatorships of the left and those of the right: To start with, those of the left keep people fenced in and watched over all the time, because

158

almost all of them would like to flee. Because of this they only let those that the regime authorizes leave the country. It is very different in right-wing dictatorships, where all common people can leave and return freely to the country as many times as they want and without government interference, provided that they don't conspire openly against the regime.

Another great difference between left wing and right wing dictatorships is that the leftist ones completely control the buying and selling of foreign currency. Currency is only acquired if it is authorized by the regime, while in dictatorships that support free enterprise, all citizens including leftists may buy currency in banks without restriction.

Another enormous difference is that in leftists dictatorships the government takes over all of the media and monopolizes all information and opinion and they select exclusively employees that share their political ideas, as much in written press (newspapers and magazines) as in radio and television programs, in which they censor all that comes to light in the public eye, in addition to criticizing everything that is capitalist and glorifying everything that has to do with the left. This practice is very different from the dictatorships that support free enterprise, which because they are not owners of the media, do not even have access to the hiring of personnel, and it is very difficult for them to avoid unfavorable news or opinions coming to light in the public eye. And although there may be acute confrontations, they make certain opposition to the dictatorship, which negatively influences its popularity, just as the decisions that it makes or stops making endanger its stability and economic progress.

Finally, we have nationalist, populist, interventionist, and anti-Yankee military officials that nationalize banks, foreign businesses, and take over or permit the invasion of land and the disrespect for private property. These

159

dictatorships create a lot of confusion and distrust, and they are a complete failure (like Chavez).

However, many media outlets damage the now rare right-wing dictatorships that are the most benevolent and neglect to criticize the most tyrannical dictatorships of the left. We can also say when they refer to dictators, they call those on the right "dictators", but they call those on the left, who are even more tyrannical, "presidents." While in anticommunist dictatorships they publicly deny economic successes and social achievements, and they even launch long campaigns to overthrow them, they hide the crimes, social and economic failures of leftist dictatorships, and even make propaganda for them.

Today we know of many changes that occurred in leftist dictatorships, above all in the economic aspect. Openness to foreign investment is the most important. It was the evident scientific and technological backwardness, like the shortage of the most essential goods and food products that made them change in their ways. Also, they realized that they could not continue lying to their flock, and continue blaming their problems on the capitalists. Circumstances obligated them to change and adopt capitalist means of production. In very little time the openness to the free market and to foreign investors has given much fruit. China has converted itself into a great power, the standard of living increases day by day and today it is one of the principal exporting countries of the world. But it continues to be a dictatorship, which shows that maybe the most important thing for progress, apart from political stability and personal security, is respect for private property, and freedom for businesses and people to create, contract, produce, trade and direct their businesses with little government interference. The failure or success of the economy depends on all of the economic policies they adopt and the confidence these policies generate in the supporters of the free marked and of free enterprise. We can not say the same of democracies, that by the sole fact of being a democracy they do not guarantee economic success.

DAMAGES OF THE GUERRILLAS

Sixty thousand dead in Hiroshima and forty thousand in Nagasaki were the cost of the only two atomic bombs launched upon humanity. And still today more than 50 years later the media reminds us of it. However, these deaths were not in vain; they caused the surrender of Japan so that the Second World War could end, which saved millions of people from deaths that would have occurred if the war had continued.

However, guerillas killed more than two hundred thousand people in Colombia alone, more than double the number of deaths caused by the bombs at Hiroshima and Nagasaki, and that is apart from the inhumane kidnappings and the thousands of injured and disappeared. And all this occurred without the least recognition. So many dead and disappeared people! So many valuable people that chose to leave! So many abandoned fields! So many businesses shattered by dejection! And even still, despite all of this, Colombia progressed. The Colombian people are to be admired! The free enterprise system that produced progress even in the midst of this tragedy is to be admired! But, how much more modern, beautiful, and developed would Colombia be if these guerillas had not existed? Fortunately guerillas tend to disappear. We refer to them in order to remember the damages they cause to countries of free enterprise. Fortunately these groups in Colombia are almost annihilated. Above all this has been done by the government presided over by Uribe, one of the most-loved presidents of the Colombian people, and now by the president Santos. However, it was then that the media intentionally worried itself over coming to an agreement with the defeated, perhaps even more worried about the fates of the guerilla leaders, than about all those who found themselves kidnapped or disappeared, who, unfortunately were most probably murdered. And why did the media remain for so many years with arms crossed permitting these grave damages and the useless genocide caused by the Marxist guerillas? Why did they not support the United States –who seemed like the only ones that worried about the situation- in the fight against the guerillas and narcotraffickers? Perhaps because they called themselves the people's armies and did everything in the name of the people, they were given the right to murder, kidnap, and try to bring everyone into the most modern form of slavery? The poor countries where this "liberation" arrived: Ethiopia, South Yemen, Angola, Cambodia, Vietnam, North Korea, Cuba, all were condemned to live in a prison regime of complete obedience and despotism, incapable of feeding itself and providing the least freedom to its people. No one could blame those who defended these groups that financed themselves with something as deplorable as drug trafficking and kidnapping people who they killed when they did not comply with their demands. It is not possible that a people that loves liberty, independence, their way of live, their religion, their property, turns its country over and agrees to slavery without protest or even a drop of blood. No one should remain with arms crossed contemplating the enormous damages of Marxist guerillas. And this is because the damages are not only in countries where they operate, but also in all countries where drugs are bought. It is a complete tragedy.

But the self-preservation instinct is innate in all living things that exist on the earth, including human beings. We all have the sacred right to defend ourselves. We all have the sacred right to defend ourselves from evil and the aggression of others. No one could be to blame for the damage that occurs to another when he acts in self-defense. And even more so when it has to do with defending oneself against atrocities that are committed in cold blood and without justification by guerillas and Marxist terrorists. This was the case in Colombian society: that while governments did very little, or tried to do very little to repress and do away with these criminals, in part perhaps because they couldn't respond with the same methods by which the criminals themselves operate, because they should respect the law and the Constitution. Colombian society upon seeing itself

163

unprotected by the government saw itself as obligated to act in self-defense, and created commands paid to combat these criminals that they did in the name of self defense, or paramilitary groups, that in the same way as the guerillas acted at the margins of the law. But that marginally legal action, without a doubt, was produced as a consequence of the guerillas so people might defend themselves from the actions of the guerillas. The most unjust thing is that in a democracy there is no motive to initiate guerrilla movements, much less to kidnap and murder, because democracies are rich in freedoms and opportunities for all. It is in totalitarian countries where guerillas can be justified, because there the opposition doesn't even have the right to an opinion or the right to spread its ideas. However, it was common to observe the media be tolerant with the Marxist guerrillas, while condemning the self-defense mechanisms created to defend against the guerillas. They have even gone so far as to attribute crimes to the defenders that were really committed by Marxist guerillas. They also interviewed very few people who were in agreement with defending themselves in some way from the guerillas.

MILITARY DEMOCRATS

The whole world knows that right wing military dictatorships are provisional, they are almost always short, and by their own evolution, they end in democracy again. Military men see the necessity of implementing them in order to keep the enemies of democracy and private property from destroying the country by taking all the powers for themselves so that they can impose true and eternal Marxist dictatorships with their ruthless censorship, repression, fear and terror. And we say "military democrats," because upon saving their countries from the worst of the dictatorships, they save democracy in their country and in neighboring countries. Let us give recognition where it's due to the Honduran people and military that bravely acted in time. Let's hope that in other countries military democrats act in time, like they did in Honduras. Fortunately the armed forces of this small country were not yet in the service of the future dictator and acted in time, before they were thrown out or made servants as have occurred in Venezuela.

However we observe, as in some countries, supposed "democrats" that put effort into punishing their ex heads of state for having had the good will and the courage to save their countries from the true and eternal enemies of democracy. They put effort into punishing those who, after having pacified, transformed and brought about progress in their country, gave up power in order to permit the return of democracy, through which they demonstrated that they did not have ambitions of power, and that they did it all out of love for their people and of freedom. This was the case with Pinochet in Chile, initially detained in another country for supposed human rights violations, and also the case of Fujimori in Peru for the same supposed reasons. Meanwhile, so many terrorists, murderers and human rights violators such as Fidel and Gadhafi (who recently was eliminated by his own people) have passed throughout the world and continue to do so, and no one detains them in order to take them to jail.

165

The whole world will agree to condemn kidnappers and terrorists that have cost the world many innocent victims. But it is illogical and absurd to condemn those who saved their countries from the claws of communism and return their countries to peace and prosperity. All wars have their dead and disappeared, and if they did not confront the enemy, the enemy would have done away with them. The communists would have done away with them surely, as they have never respected human rights, or treaties of any kind.

Those who make an effort to condemn these ex heads of state cannot be democrats. They must be at the service of the enemies of democracy. Then, who wanted to condemn those who deserved to be decorated for saving their countries from the true enemies of democracy? Who would want to punish those who complied with the sacred task of defending their country, stopping the communists from remaining in power? Who but the communists would want to punish those whose countrymen are thanking them for having taken over the helm of the country and steered it out of the ruin in which it was left by the leftists? Who are those who really make an effort to punish these patriots? It appears that they want to leave their countries adrift and without defense against totalitarian communism, but they should think twice before giving power to those who could very well be their executioners.

And to top it all off we see see magistrates and governors who boast that they are "democrats", on one hand, but who try to condemn those who saved their countries from the worst of tyrannies while on the other hand they try to negotiate and leave in liberty the guerrilla leaders and terrorists, the true murderers and enemies of democracy. This is what the world is coming to.

THE FRAGILE DEMOCRACY

We don't have the smallest doubt that democracy is the best system of government. But because of the many liberties that it permits, it is now also the most difficult, complex, and vulnerable form of government. There is not a period of government as good as it may be, when everyone is in agreement with the government, so therefore there is always opposition. It is the only type of government that by its very nature is constantly submitted, day after day and year after year, to the criticisms and pressures of all sectors of the country: political, economic, social, environmental, cultural, etc. This is the very essence of the democratic system, since it is these criticisms, when they are made in good faith and with the intention of bringing about solutions, that day after day perfect and produce more security and well-being to the greatest degree for its population in the best environment of freedom and respect for the law. Unfortunately, many times the enemies of private property do not criticize in order to bring about solutions, but rather to damage the system. We should be cognizant of the fact that authentic democracies can only coexist with free enterprise, and that the most noble of these is to try to perfect from the bottom up, looking for better security and well-being for all. Unfortunately not everyone gets this well-being because it is held back by the very deficiencies of democracy, among which is that of permitting enemies in its own backyard whose interest is not in perfecting democracy, but rather in damaging it in order to facilitate their own take-over of power.

One of the very good things that genuine democracies have is that laws are made by the very citizens themselves, and for that reason the citizens are the only ones that can change their way of life. Democracies are places where everyone has a right to exhibit their ideas and to reject or accept those of others, or to express satisfaction or discontent with something without fear of any type.

167

But it is vitally important for whatever legislative project that it is discussed widely in public, with the same opportunities for those who are in favor as for those who are against it, so that everyone can later decide in fair elections to either accept the project or not.

In democracy, public employees, including the president, are public servants. They should limit themselves to performing well the functions that they are elected to perform. They should be conscious of the fact that they are paid to protect citizens from what is undesirable, like delinquents and unfit politicians. They are never to impose changes on citizens' way of life, much less to dispossess them of their belongings, which is an even more serious crime than if a criminal were to do it out of necessity.

Public employees are elected and paid in order to facilitate things for citizens, never to hold things up, make things worse, cause inflation, or make things more difficult for them. And public employees are the first who should comply with laws and the constitution.

Things are very different in dictatorships, where there are no worthy laws, and where the citizens are always subjugated to the functionaries. And when they have elections it is only to trick the people and create a semblance of democracy.

In democracy, all political acts should be public, so that each person has the right to know the truth about what the politicians propose to do. Because it is only possible to make really beneficial changes when all the projects and ideas are based in truth, because when people vote after having been tricked, the vote is no longer the will of the people. And citizens just as much as the media should have access at all moments to voting centers so that the whole nation can observe the process. And in the referendums, every faction should have the same quantity of representatives at the voting tables and where the votes are being counted.

On the other hand, all political movements of whichever kind that employs dishonest methods to win supporters should be eradicated, and those responsible brought to justice. We should never permit groups or parties rooted in crime. And we should never justify evil for the sake of arriving at a good end. We should be teaching this by example. A blow to the head kills the snake. This has been the great farce of the enemies of free enterprise for while they violate the law constantly, in the most terrible and underhanded way, they want the rest of us to obey.

Let us imagine for a moment that all politicians acted in good faith, recognizing the good and criticizing the bad in order to correct it, and contributing to the perfecting of the system in order to better serve the community. How would democracies be then if instead of damages they received support? They would be even better, considering the capacity of the free enterprise system to recuperate from the damages that are intentionally done to it. It is not that even more perfect democracies will get rid of problems. This is something that they will never be able to avoid. But without a doubt the problems will be greatly reduced.

Unfortunately many democracies succumb because of lack of defenses. For that reason it is necessary to possess the media, because its influence is very great in terms of influencing voters and politicians, upon whom the future of all citizens stands. Because if the media falls into the hands of the left, all the economic and political power in the world will fall irredeemably into its hands.

WHO ARE THE CORRUPT?

Those who have had the opportunity to visit countries with leftist totalitarian regimes, or observe their streets in movies or photographs will have been able to observe the meager quantity of vehicles (although things are now changing due to foreign investment). Seeing few cars is not by chance, as we could easily suppose. It is a simple matter because the great majority or people do not have the money to acquire them.

Well then, these vehicles being so necessary, wouldn't people be more tempted to get money illicitly that would help them obtain even the most insignificant of the automobiles? What holds them back from criminal actions? Why is there not more corruption among the marginal classes in these countries? Some of the reasons are in the first place, because of the strict vigilance exercised over every person. In the second place, because of fear of the regime and or being denounced. In the third place, because of the strict moral controls under their views. And in the fourth and most important reason, because of the severe punishments that include the death penalty. By contrast, among the leaders there is much corruption. But the slaves do not realize it because there is no freedom of expression, because the media is controlled by the high officials, because there is no one keeping an eye on the journalists, nor the denunciations of the citizens, nor the other political parties that could have been attentive to these irregularities as occurs in free countries. Something very different occurs in true democracies, where the high officials are submitted to a higher vigilance in all sectors, and the citizens can denounce corruption without the fear that exists in dictatorships.

There should be less corruption in countries with a free enterprise system, because people can make money in varying ways and raise their standard of living. For this reason they are always thinking of what to sell, or what service to provide, or what to invent that people will like or find a use for. And even in playing the lottery. And it is because of this that free countries are always stuffed with things to buy. In contrast, in leftist dictatorial regimes, the biggest worry of the people is, simply, what can we buy with the money they give us? And on not having the same ways that exist in free countries to bring up their standard of living, they should have a greater temptation to be corrupt in order to obtain what they desire, provided they can get it. What we want to make clear is that in leftist regimes there is more of an incentive to take money wrongfully. That in public administration it is easier to take funds illicitly because there is no one who will suffer because of their loss. And as more businesses and offices are administered by public officials, there will be a greater risk of corruption. It could seem to us that there is more corruption at the upper levels in democratic countries, but it is because in the totalitarian regimes it is rarely made public, and the people do not realize it. Let us not forget that in dictatorships the only acts of corruption that are made known are the ones the government wants us to know about. And if the people internally do not realize, the people who are outside can figure it out even less.

Lack of a good moral, civic, and religious background influences corruption as well. But without a doubt, what is most influential is the lack of severe punishments, because if punishments were more severe, criminals wouldn't then see their actions as acts of cunning, but rather as serious crimes. Without a doubt, the fear of punishment causes people to avoid corruption and leftist totalitarian regimes punish severely. So much so that serious cases include the death penalty and it is a serious crime for an administrator at a shirt factory to take or sell some of the product to keep the money, something that in a free country, if the act was even punished, it would only lead to the administrator being fired. If free countries were to adopt the same punishments, all people would become conscious that corruption is a grave crime, and then it would disappear. This effect of the fear of punishment can also be observed in right-wing military dictatorships, in which there is also little crime.

171

Corruption also has little to do with deprivation, as some would suppose. The most palpable test is that the majority of the corrupt are well-paid functionaries, and they do not know what it is like to be hungry or in need. Let us remember that in free countries there are very few leftists who identify themselves as such, and they are in all parties and in all governments.

Corruption also happens in the private sector, but the cases are much more isolated because of the vigilance that the owners exercise. But the most spectacular corruption happens in developing countries, above all in petroleum exporters, which have almost all been underhandedly taken over by the enemies of free enterprise. The ideology that they profess with their immoral practices permits them to rob everything they can without conscience. They are criminals helped by a type of permanent complicity of the media that favors forgetfulness, without there being justice. They are vulgar con men who should be in jail today if it were not for this "society of accomplices" within the media who turn a blind eye. Legitimate private business survives against the prevailing corruption. There are many new millionaires given placements as owners of large businesses, among them banks and above all the media, but these businesses were bought of founded with ill-gotten funds, the great majority, from oil-exporting countries in the hands of the left. For the true businessman to be associated with these thieves is like blaming the farmers for the cattle or money that they had to pay the guerrillas with, so that they would not be kidnapped (the so called vaccine).

The other reality about the outward flow of currency is that much of the private savings of small and medium sized savings accounts, just as that of the large businesses, goes out of the country because people want to put part of their savings away safely for the future of their children, because all the political and economic disasters caused by the public administration. It is a simple act of the self-preservation instinct. These savings, in addition to the fact that they would never go if the conditions in the country were safe, also would return if people believed that they had the adequate conditions of security and confidence.

LACK OF SECURITY: WHO IS TO BLAME?

Who is to blame for our problems? Two hundred years ago Bolivar said to use "Clemency with a criminal is an attack on virtue." "Corruption of the people is born of the indulgence of the tribunals and the impunity of the crimes. Without force there is no virtue and without virtue the republic suffers."

In effect, delinquency is not the lack of budgeting, or of police, or of equipment. The great problem is impunity and the lack of severe punishments that are respected. And such punishment doesn't cost the citizens a cent. On the contrary, it would save them a lot of money because they wouldn't need many jails, equipment, or police.

There are countries where they cut off the hand of those who steal. However, no one sees a one-handed man in the street. They simply do not rob. In many countries people have severe laws and dissuasive punishments that protect them from thieves and criminals. In others however, it is the delinquents that have laws to protect them and even serve to keep them in liberty. On the other hand, for those people who are honest and hard-working, their human rights do not exist. Delinquents do not only take their lives, but they also kidnap them, depriving them of liberty and even their own life savings. And no one runs out to defend the rights that supposedly we all should have to live and work in peace. And a diligent authority figure ready to confront the wrongdoings scarcely emerges and, as if by magic, defenders of human rights come out from among the delinquents. But, why would it be that this only happens in countries where the means of production are in private hands? It is a great injustice that in these countries the punishment is only for the honest and hard-working people who try to survive in an environment filled with danger, corruption, and immorality. Even the police who are charged with keeping order and public security are corrupt, a result of the same impunity or lack of authority and punishment. We reap what we sow.

174

Neither is delinquency a consequence of poverty, as some would justify it. For example: everyone knows of the many scarcities and necessities that happen to people in dictatorships of the proletariat, as in that of Fidel in Cuba. According to that hypothesis, delinquency should have proliferated, however that is not the case, because there is an iron fist for delinquents. There was also little crime in the military dictatorships of the right as in that of Franco in Spain, Perez Jimenez in Venezuela, and Pinochet in Chile. But later –despite the known prosperity that these countries experienced during those dictatorships- upon the arrival of democracy and with it the enemies of private property, delinquency came to proliferate again as a consequence of the lack of authority and punishment. There are parents who want the best for their children, who love them more than anyone, who please them in everything, who do not assign them chores nor do they punish all the bad things they do so as not to have conflict with them, or because they are afraid that their child will become angry or ill-willed, and they even justify their bad actions and defend them before everyone else. And what are the results? Generally they get the opposite of what they expected from their children, which can become a serious problem even for their own parents: the children do not respect them, they yell at them, and they even go so far as to hit them. Conversely those parents that also love their children a lot, but base the children's education of the experience of others, act almost completely the other way: they please their children only when they see it as convenient. Despite the children's complaints, they instruct them and make them work. They teach them to be organized and disciplined, they punish their bad actions, and they do not justify the things they do poorly. The result is a successful relationship between parents and children. And these children love their parents more and are grateful their entire lives for having been raised in an environment of order, obedience, work and discipline.

The same happens in governing a country, which is like a large family, and the people that have the responsibility of directing it, legislating or influencing in the form of education, discipline and treatment of its citizens are like representatives of this large family, and when they fail, the family fails, the whole country fails. The governors did things in reverse: they tried to please the whole world. They legislated so that all people would work less and would receive more. They forgot about morality and good manners. They did not worry about discipline or good education. They justified the delinquency and disrespect for private property in the name of marginality. And crime was punished very little.

Crime proliferates when there is little punishment and it becomes the easiest way of getting money or power, and even more so knowing that the police, for the same motives, exploit their own business. Let's look at an example: an honest official detains a delinquent, who then offers him money to set him free. The official does not accept the bribe and turns the man over to justice. However, in a few days he realizes that this criminal is free. The official, in the same way as any of us if we were in his place, will ask himself: what was my effort, my honor and the risk I took good for? What was the point, except to gain myself an enemy? In the end he is still on the loose, and I would have money instead of an enemy. As we can well appreciate, the policeman fulfilled his duty by arresting the criminal but it was in vain. Who was really punished? Who would not be demoralized when there is no punishment for the wicked, but instead there is one for the good? And it doesn't have to do with just sporadic cases, this happens in many countries. It would be very different in Venezuela and in other countries with respect to delinquency and lack of personal security if we had taken into account Bolivar's thoughts. Here are some: "...the health of a Republic depends on morals that citizens acquire through education in their childhood." "Teaching about good manners or social graces is as essential as instruction..." "Impunity for crimes makes people commit them more frequently: at the end we get to the point where the punishment is not enough to suppress them."

THE DEATH PENALTY: WHO USES IT?

We should be clear: When justice works well, capital punishment is not necessary. What happens is that unfortunately, in some countries, instead of being a society that condemns delinquents, it is these same delinquents (including kidnappers, guerrillas, and terrorists) that condemn honest people to death without distinguishing by sex or age; they could be women, children, or the elderly. In addition, this is done the majority of the time with impunity. Conversely in these same countries, decent, honorable, hard-working people cannot condemn these depraved criminals who cause so much physical, mental and moral damage. Punishing these criminals would cause a half dozen to die in a year, but these delinquents would let thousands of innocent people be murdered. Because we all know that the death penalty is not applied because it is cruel, but rather it exists in order to dissuade; for this reason in countries where the death penalty is used there are very few crimes.

Where would human behavior sink to if rewards and punishments did not exist?

All human actions, even religious actions, are based in reward and punishment. If one walks on a good path he will be rewarded; if on the contrary he walks on a bad path he will be punished. Christian religions teach us that if we die in sin we will pay for it in eternal fire. Could there be a more severe punishment? They condemn us to suffer eternally the flames of Hell. Even, if we analyzed it from the practical and religious point of view, when society condemns a delinquent to death, they do him a great favor, because they give him the opportunity to repent and save himself from the eternal flames of Hell. This is an opportunity that lamentably honest people do no have when they are condemned and executed by the delinquents. Neither is the command "Thou shall not kill" contradictory, because with it we avoid repeated violation of the commandment. It is not the same that once in awhile a delinquent dies after having been judged by the

Law, when thousands of times this command is profaned by delinquents, guerrillas, and terrorists murdering innocent people all year long, either individually or in groups.

An organized and modern society also needs severe punishments that are respected. Unfortunately there will always exist those who oppose severe punishments because as Bolivar said so well two centuries ago "...the thief is always fearful of justice."

But, why does the media only criticize the death penalty in capitalist countries? Why does it not criticize that which exists in all leftist dictatorships?

Who could not affirm that there exists no greater security than when a delinquent in incinerated or buried, that when he is imprisoned we run the risk of him escaping or being unjustly liberated and continuing to kill innocent people, as has happened so many times? Additionally, the taxpayers would not have to feed him or maintain him indefinitely at their own cost and through their own work. Even, if we conduct a survey, we could realize that the majority of people agree with more severe punishments for delinquents, including the death penalty in some cases. And if democracy is to do the will of the people, why then do they not fulfill the people's will?

And at the end of the short dictatorship of Perez Jimenez, the Venezuelans enjoyed prosperity, full employment, medical assistance and free medicines, unlimited and free education, good lines of communication, eradication of poor housing in favor of comfortable apartments, personal security and very little crime. Did this prosperity stop the proliferation of crime as a consequence of the lack of punishment or impunity that followed with the arrival of "democracy" and of the leftists?

A few years ago, as always occurs when leftists take power, poverty increased greatly in China. And why did

179

crime and corruption not proliferate in that country? Often we find out about some cases of delinquency and corruption in China through the media: "Three suspects who attacked a valuable goods transport were hanged", "Corrupt functionary executed in such-and-such province of China." How could crime proliferate with such examples and dissuasive punishments? And are they perhaps not in the right? Perhaps it is not preferable for it to be society that eliminates a depraved delinquent every once in awhile that where the delinquents are the ones who impose the death penalty on whoever they see fit three hundred and sixty five days a year?

Paradoxically in countries that have free enterprise, every time the community is worried about the serious security situation, they propose reforms of laws to impose severe punishments that include the death penalty, the first to oppose them are the leftists. Yes sir. They come out immediately from their respective and influential positions to oppose the reforms. The 99 percent of people who scream for reforms are of little importance to them. They always have some stupid argument at hand. These unique people that stop delinquents from being punished in democracies, and attack those who propose sanctions that are respected, are precisely those who are most responsible for crime, and the deaths of innocents, generalized corruption, and lack of personal safety.

Upon permitting a deranged criminal to continue in liberty, we cause a problem for the whole world. For this reason, the best politician searches out and locks up the criminal.

180

WHO IS TO BLAME FOR OUR TROUBLES?

It seems unusual that at these heights of the 21st century, when the world should already have solutions for almost all its economic and social problems, there is still crisis, senseless terrorism, and much need. For example: Venezuela, with one of the largest currency income in the world in proportion with its inhabitants, should be the country with the highest quality of living in the world, a very solid currency, with immense reserves, and no debt of course. It was the dictatorship of Perez Jimenez, when leftist activists were exiled or operating in hiding, when the Venezuelans saw progress and great works, and sold petroleum at less than two dollars a barrel. But after 1958, with populist and interventionist leftist governments, despite having received immense quantities of dollars because of the high oil prices, the country fell back, and as the icing on the cake, it became scandalously indebted. And what were the tactics that characterized these governments? Let's mention a few: 1) Financing political parties and unions with which they promoted idleness and confrontation, 2) To tolerate and demand commissions or bribes from the purchases and projects contracted by political functionaries, for which they became first among the corrupt and the corruptors, 3) Instituting a beaurocracy consumed by foods and goods, but at the same time incapable of producing them, 4) Lack of punishment and systematic weakness for dealing with criminals, justifying them as "victims of the system," which brought as a consequence a proliferation of delinquency, lack or security in all parts and waste of a great deal of material and human resources in security and protection, 5) inexistence of measures aimed at curbing immorality and elevating civic behavior, which caused moral deterioration and breakdown of the family and society, 6) Interventionism in the economy, including suspension of economic guaranties sometimes, and obstacles to the free market with the inevitable slowing down of production, in addition to the profound unease and lack of enthusiasm in the collective, an

181

indispensible factor in the progress of a country, 7) Nationalization of businesses, which made foreign investors flee, those who had produced wealth, technology, and well-being, 8) implementation of laws and terrible labor rules, that instead of incentivizing production and work, incited bad behavior, laziness, and irresponsibility in work and also produced confrontations, 9) Blind and undue protectionism for industries installed in the country, creating monopolies of manufacturers and importers protected by the governments, and obligating the people to buy at prices that were much higher than usual, 10) Promoting and tolerating the invasions of rural and urban lands, inciting disorder, violating the right to property, and provoking the discouragement of production, all of which generated a lack of productivity, disinvestment, shortage of goods and food products, 11) constant devaluations of currency by which the people became more and more impoverished, so that there are more dollars for the functionaries to use for themselves, take and invest in their own ill born business. Upon reflecting on these and other terrible policies caused and tolerated by leftists, and added to the human and material losses that are irreparable and caused directly by guerrillas and terrorists, we realize perfectly who is responsible for our problems, as much in Venezuela as in other countries. Added to the rest, it is said that the government that has received the most money and has caused the most damage is that of Chavez.

The big problem is that we continue confusing many young students, to whom, instead of teaching them the good of the free enterprise system, we portray it as an unjust system, so that later these young people, believing that they know the secret of our problems, dedicate their lives to slow down the development of the country and to generate more poverty.

WHEN THE NORTH AMERICANS EXPLOITED US

And who better than an ex-petroleum industry worker to narrate the coexistence between Venezuelans and North Americans when they possessed and administrated the petroleum industry?

The article below that you will read was published in a Venezuelan newspaper halfway through 1982, and here we reproduced part of it with the permission of its author: R.A. Pampolini.

The Near Paradise on Earth in Venezuela   By: R.A. Pampolini

It is a moral obligation to recognize and a sin to fail to recognize something good and give thanks to its creator.

When man comes to realize a work that by its beauty, functionality, and genius elevates human life, he completes a holy action. It is just, then, to make it known with the end of motivating and incentivizing others. It is good and noble to pay our debt to him who has given us so much.

Here I am today, to describe something unprecedented which refers to the time when I had the good fortune to live an interesting experience: that of working for a company: CREOLE PETROLEUM CORPORTATION in the area of La Salina (CABIMAS) on the East Coast of Maracaibo Lake, Zulia state, Venezuela.

It was a true revelation and beautiful surprise to observe the good of the petroleum camps "Hollywood" and "Las Cupulas," their functional houses, not luxurious but pretty, and their well-constructed streets, well maintained, and with the grass always trimmed, with landscaping of all types around the houses. Essential services like light, water, gas, and telephone were administered with precise efficiency, but above all with functionality, and were reliable. In the 5 years that I have the good fortune to live in "Las Cupulas," I never lacked services except for one time and that was only for a few hours.

The American organization, typical of CREOLE, showed its talents in constructing areas so that man could live a dignified and fruitful life.

Man, whose gift of life should contribute to the happiness of mankind, had in his grasp everything necessary to develop for himself his own environment.

An area that pleased me was the patio of the central workshops. Large and spacious, level, well constructed with asphalt. Nice fans twirled on the rooftop; they seemed like large spirits of God with their blades in perpetual rotation... American men know how to plan, they know about engineering in rural areas, and they also know about poetry. I always said that it was the best I had seen in my life. The patio of the Central Workshops was the most beautiful area designed for and by man. It was so functional that it was pleasing even to drive a car through its corners. A shop on the right hand side was filled with lots of mechanical and electrical equipment in organized scaffoldings, under constant fresh ventilation, that made it pleasant to look for a spare part in those stores. The organization of the warehouse, the courtesy of the staff, and the quick and sure references, the certainty of finding the right part, everything about it made us look with fondness on the great warehouse of the CREOLE.

At the entrance were the electrical service workshops and it was also pleasant to enter those. One noted efficiency, space, and functionality. There was much courtesy between Venezuelans and North Americans along with a great desire to collaborate and excellent human relations. The North Americans won the hearts of the Venezuelans and vice versa.

Both esteemed and appreciated one another; going to work with them was a privilege.

At six thirty in the morning no one was absent from work.

And upon returning to camp, after so many interesting endeavors at work, one felt in harmony with God. At night, the camp with its lights and its beautiful streets, invited rest, meet-ups, and communication. The community of CREOLE was truly a place of God. The children coming back from school gave us certainty about the future: a great future. The schools were beautiful and functional. The central school of Las Cupulas was a dream of a primary school. Space, light, classes, atmosphere, pedagogical equipment, seats, blackboards, etc. Everything well designed and organized. Here organization was synonymous with beauty, functionality, and efficiency. Blessed Americans, how they knew these things...they left the best they could create in those camps, so useful for a happy life. It was so easy to visit the residents of the community. That was another great advantage of life in the camp.

It was pleasant to meet up at a friend's house, chat and drink as well. If not, to the club, just a few hundred meters away. It wasn't worth the trouble to go in a car. One arrived on foot to the La Salina Club, with its facilities at the service of the workers and families of CREOLE. Conferences, chats, cinema, study, reading, bowling, tennis, a pool, everything at the user's hand. The cleaning service was always at the attention of the business that maintained clean, beautiful, agreeable streets just like the facilities of the club. What an example of efficiency we learned in the community with the North Americans. They were men of stature, not only physically but also morally. Reliable, serious, attentive, and at your service. To ask a favor to a "Musiu" was to do a pleasant thing: I'm very glad to please you...and to the most cultured... yes sir...let me help you...so the gringa women

185

also said to us, with the will to serve. When will we return to having an amiable and harmonized life like that?

The most creative and evocative Christmas times of the spirit of the baby Jesus were those of the years that we lived with the gringos of CREOLE company. The camps were filled with lights and Christmas motifs, every house with its little trees and its wreaths. Jingle Bells and Silent Night floating with their musical notes and the stars in the Christmas Trees in every house. A smooth sky of Christmas Eve, making the environment at the highest point of the camps in perfect harmony with the happiness of the recurrence of Christmas. The different "tongues" under the sky of the Baby Jesus did not make a difference; a good man is a friend to all, and the gringos and locals lived in peace, celebrating the luck of being sons of God. Pleasant memories were those that I will take with me for eternity. The brotherhood we lived out in the petroleum camps. We should not forget that humanity could be happy if it knew how to be brotherly, if it knew how to recognize the good in everyone, if it knew how to tolerate defects and above all to appreciate all good things that are common to all men. We should work so that the great experience of coexistence between different peoples as it was realized in the CREOLE petroleum camps is not lost. That the importance of living together and permitting the development of talent is profoundly analyzed, just as it occurred with men of the North who found out how to give us a model, a norm of how we could live in almost perfect community. To copy and meditate on what occurred among those men is our challenge. It will not be easy to achieve such great results. That is the truth, but we should make every effort to realize it.

The North Americans had seen it achieved in Europe, when they arrived to Italy at the end of the Second World War, full of friendship and love for their suffering neighbors, armed only with a great hope and nobility in their hearts, and the capacity and enthusiasm to help others and participate with their possessions and their wills to live.

186

THIRD PART

ON THE PATH TO A WORLD OF TYRANNY?

THE SILENT THIRD WAR

Although many do not believe it, it is being fought right now. And the saddest part is that few realize why there is no information about what is occurring. And there is no information because the enemies of private property, empowered not by chance by the media, have no interest in spreading it. "A war noticed in advance doesn't kill any soldiers." And they continue stockpiling the media outlets: the most effective weapons of this war. And it is not by force, it is in the simplest way: they buy them or install new media outlets. And although many would not believe it, they already underhandedly control the majority of television channels at a world level, in addition to radio, newspapers and magazines with which they obtain every day more power to confuse, manipulate, and brainwash at their convenience, with a biased and generalized opinion that would give them access to all powers, even within the United States. And on getting it, they will have won the Third World War, and all of the countries would become territories of a sole empire. We are then at the edge of an abyss, with the media subjugating our minds, which they use to control our bodies and convert us into what they want. They have even gone so far as to make television documentaries in Spanish in order to make it seem to many people that the Twin Towers did not fall because of terrorist acts, instead that they were meticulously loaded with explosives and blown up by the government of the United States. Just a short time ago we saw a "great report" by the History Channel in Spanish where, in summary, they want people to believe that the government of the United States by various methods can now produce hurricanes, earthquakes, and even great droughts, which now could be used as devastating weapons against its enemies, among which were Iran and North Korea mentioned. And this is extremely serious because unfortunately many people let themselves be manipulated easily by the media and do not realize that the purpose of these reports is to sew hate against the United

States and to justify even more terrorism. Surely this channel has also passed into the hands of the enemy.

Whether it has to do with political, social, economic, or religious themes, we can now read, watch, or hear almost only information and opinion that the enemy wants us to. They manipulate information. They manipulate polls. And they control the opinion by interviewing only people from the left, only their own "analysts" including supposed businessmen that are only figureheads of the left. Conversely, they do not interview those that defend the free enterprise system, even though they may be 99 percent of the population. Naturally, when people only hear, see, or read the opinion of the enemy, though they may think correctly and are part of the 99 percent, they can come to believe that everyone thinks that way, that they are the only ones who are mistaken, and with few exceptions they come to act and think how the enemy wants them to. And in order to spread it, they could interview once in awhile someone who opposes them, but always cutting out what they don't want people to read, hear, or see. And when the program is live, they limit that person to answering only questions that the network has selected. And if the interviewee touches on a theme that hurts them, they interrupt him or ask other questions to change the subject.

Unfortunately, they can omit, distort, exaggerate, hide or manipulate all information at their convenience. They are even going so far as to distort the Bible, which they interpret in their own way. They also manipulated almanacs and even definitions contained in some dictionaries. Although, if we are conscious of what is occurring, it will be more difficult to let ourselves be manipulated. We will conserve then our old history and religious books that could serve as a moral and spiritual guide, because the leftists changed the meanings and facts in the new editions. We cannot sit idly by. It is necessary to detain the hoarding of the media influence. In the countries where we are still able, where they still have not taken over all powers, every business with enough economic power that has not yet been bought by the enemies of private property should start up their own television channel, radio station, or found a newspaper. We should denounce what is occurring without fear of failure, because the bad has never prevailed against the good. The truth will always triumph over lies. The people are sick of trickery, manipulation, and immorality, of wolves in sheep's clothing in public offices, of demons dressed as priests that commit all kinds of aberrations. But it is still possible to change things. It is our moral obligation, to comment on and spread knowledge of this grotesque crime against all humanity. Enough with monopolizing the most important media outlets, as well as the principal editorials and book distributors. It is now difficult to find books that denounce the horrors of communism and defend the free enterprise system. We urge you to find confirmation by looking for them in bookstores. And if they continue stockpiling media influence, like publishers, book distributors, and even the greater part of the Internet, probably within a short time, world power could be within their grasp. Our future is at stake, that of our families and of all of humanity.

THE WEAPONS: THE MEDIA

If a photograph and a few commentaries about the deterioration of a city street is emphasized on the front page of the newspaper, it is enough to cause it to be fixed immediately. The same occurs when it has to do with more important subjects like passing or reforming a law. For bad or good, the influence of the media is decisive for passing, accelerating, tabling, or denying any legislative project. The media has so much power that in a country where freedom of expression exists, they can bring whomever they want to the presidency of a country, just as they can also take away the presidency. A good example of this power is when they made President Nixon of the United States resign. We can affirm that in practice, all the powers of government together cannot equal the great power and influences of the media.

We all like to be well informed, but those who have important charges like presidents, governors, mayors, judges, congressmen, commanders of the armed forces and other political leaders, union leaders, employers, or religious figureheads, will always be more interested in reading the news and opinions that appear daily in the media. Rare will be the day that they begin their activities before reading the information and opinion of the main newspapers of their country. With the same interest they will be watching the main television news channels. As the simple mortals that they are, they need to know what is said, kept quiet, exalted or criticized in the media. And the critiques and commentaries of their own negotiations or actions will be the deciding factor for the greater part of the next decisions that they make.

Two hundred years ago, when radio and television did not exist and media outlets were very scarce, Bolivar expressed "The first of all forces is public opinion." Currently the media is the first of all forces and it is responsible for making public opinion. The media is a more powerful and effective weapon than nuclear missiles, since nuclear weapons are kept locked up, but the media acts constantly upon the minds of people, the majority of which come to think and act according to the criteria presented by the media that they read, watch, or hear.

If in Russia, China, Cuba, or other countries with totalitarian leftist governments, all the media is in the hands of the government, and all the news and editorials are controlled and authorized by those dictatorial governments, why then in free countries is the media not reciprocally in the hands of the supporters of free enterprise? But to cap it all off, all these media outlets can also be bought by the enemies of free enterprise and used as a Trojan horse to take power from within. Unfortunately, this is already occurring. They already possess many media outlets that are influencing voters to put their people in the senate, presidency, governorship, and in all key political offices. The media is the principal weapon that is being used by the enemies of free enterprise in this unjust and underhanded war that is waged against free countries. There are very few media outlets in the hands of the supporters of free enterprise, and these could easily fall quickly into the hands of the Marxists. Conversely, those that have been bought or were founded by the international left will always follow their guidelines. They will never go back to the other side. They will not be permitted to. Not even when one of their leaders or figureheads becomes convinced that they are on the wrong side. This means that unless we act quickly, all of the media will be in the hands of the enemies of private property. That also means that because of the great influence that the media has, all the heads of state and functionaries that are elected from now on will also be from the left, and evidently all countries will come to be part of a sole empire.

Let's recall that the enemies of private property do not identify themselves. They do not give themselves away publicly. Because of this, media outlets are acquired under the name of figureheads, so that they people think that their owners are businessmen. For this reason the left continues confusing many people. In other words, if we do not take drastic measures urgently, it will be difficult to avoid global subjugation.

However, it is still possible to avoid it, and one way is in all countries where the Marxists have still not taken all the powers, the democrats urgently do what the left has been doing. Just as the left possesses all the media in Russia, China, Cuba, and many other countries, and no one has yet complained about this fact, with even more reason the supporters of free enterprise should possesses all media, and no one should complain. Is it perhaps just that Marxists permit themselves to take over all media in free enterprise countries, and even to make public opinion, while in countries where the Marxists govern, they don't even permit supporters of free enterprise to install even one? We believe that just as the Armed Forces are to defend a country and its citizens from its enemies, so also the media should be used to defend the country and its citizens from the enemies of freedom, truth, private property, and democracy. That just as in all countries with leftist totalitarian regimes the armed forces and the media are in the left's power, with even more reason in free countries, just as the armed forces defend against enemies, all the media should be and remain in the hands of the system of free enterprise, never in the hands of the Marxists because everything would come into their power. Because of this, with higher goals than public utility, for the survival of democracy, of free enterprise, of private property and liberty, and in order to continue being free and independent, the media should be acquired and remain at all times in the hands of the governments and journalists that appreciate and value liberty, independence, our system of government, respect for human rights, private property in the means of production, the free market and free enterprise. This is very different from the countries subjected to the Marxists where no human right is respected.

This acquisition needs to occur urgently. It has to do with getting rid of all the bad that the Marxists are creating. It

193

means saving morals and decency. It means doing away with lies and corruption. It means saving our way of life, and continuing to be free and independent.

And it's not that we want to do away with freedom of expression. Just the opposite. As we explained in "False Pluralism," what we want is to stop the enemies of democracy and free expression of thought from taking power. What we want to avoid is the enemies of truth, freedom, and plurality taking power.

And the initiative will not come from the media because almost all media outlets are in the hands of the enemies of free enterprise. The initiative should come urgently from the high military command without letting itself be influenced by those that protest. They can assure that they are enemies of private property in the means of production, service, and information. Why did they not protest and complain before, that in the countries where people are subjugated, that the governors are always reactionary leftists, and the media as well? Why then are they going to complain now that the democrats and supporters of private property and liberty want to do the same in self-defense?

To do nothing would be the same as permitting all media outlets to fall into the hands of the Marxists, to let them take world power, and to subjugate everyone. Is this what they want for their country and for the whole world? This is not a mere supposition. Neither is it a fictional movie that we know has an end, nor is it a nightmare from which we can awaken ourselves. It is already occurring at the world level.

And if the media can bring whatever person into the presidency of a country, and make the most powerful man in the world resign, could they not do the same for the system that has generated the most progress and well-being with the extraordinary merit of having done so with all of the people in freedom, and despite the enormous damages that they have had to endure from the enemy.

And if freedom of expression only exists in democratic countries with a free enterprise system, should not the media then be the staunchest defender of democracy and free enterprise?

Imagine that you are the owner of a media outlet and you know very well that the desired end of the enemies of free enterprise is to take over all the means of production and service, including the media. Would you leave out the columnists who defend private property and give priority to those who want to take it away from you? Why do the majority of media outlets do precisely that? Why to they interview supposed "analysts" at every moment, all of them from the left, and do not interview nearly as many personalities that defend private property and free enterprise? Why do they leave them out and go so far as to not even publish their writings? Perhaps we don't realize what side they are on. Why do they "forget" certain events immediately, while they use others to feed the fire?

Let us recall these wise biblical words: "By their fruits you shall know them." It is easy to know on which side they are, observing which countries they damage and which ones they try to help, which candidates they promote, and which they ignore or criticize. We can see easily if they are always watching to catch the smallest error of the heads of state of the right, while they "forget" completely the excesses of the heads of state of the left and their systematic violations of human rights. And the same thing occurs with the news. The media in the hands of the enemies of free enterprise does a lot of damage by deliberately omitting crimes and atrocities that are committed by Marxists, while they bring to the forefront the news and opinion that damages the country and the free enterprise system. Because of this, they never interview the immense quantity of personalities that defend the free enterprise system, nor their candidates for public office.

When the media is with the system of free enterprise, the information and opinion given will be completely different. It will be made with total honesty and responsibility, and with the healthiest intention of supporting solutions and helping others. And the situation in the world will be very different. We will be able to eradicate lies, crime, robbery, kidnapping, hypocrisy, corruption, and terrorism and construct a world that is more just and humane. Where the actions of the media and of the journalists will be honest, responsibly oriented toward the perfection of the democratic system, the only system the permits reporters to fulfill their role as true journalists. Without silencing the injustices or the errors of the governments because it is necessary that they are known and denounced, but constructively, in good faith, with the intention of correcting them, punishing or rewarding those who deserve it. And in order to achieve this, it will be necessary to keep an eye on all governors, functionaries and journalists so that they are proven honest, democratic, and supporters of private property and free enterprise.

BUT ARE STILL COMMUNISTS?

We all realized the failure of Marxism as a system. Marx's theories were badly supported or erroneously analyzed. Some were analyzed from only one point of view. For example: equality, exploitation of man by his fellow man, surplus value, labor stability, the concept "each according to his need," the consideration of religion as "the opiate of the masses," etc. But there is no doubt that these ideas, with their terrorizing practices of justifying whatever means to produce their ends, completely changed history. And despite the observed changes, they still kept the world in confusion. Really these ideas have not died. How could they disappear while there are still people who believe in them? In truth this would not be important; the larger problem is trying to impose them no matter what.

Although the Russians and the Chinese publicly do not admit it, it is clearly seen that what they did was simply a pause. The circumstances obligated them to change. Technological delay was evident in all areas, from agriculture to arms. The technology and progress of the western world roped them in and this made them depend more on the West. They needed to equip themselves. They needed to get that technology and by themselves they would never get it. And the easiest way to get it was to make the capitalists believe that they were throwing in the towel, to make it understood that they were abandoning Marxism and totalitarianism and that they had converted themselves into democracies and supporters of free enterprise and private property. They realized that they could never get out of the technological backwardness in which they found themselves without the financial and technological help of the West. They changed their strategy: to make Westerners believe that they had become democrats and capitalists. And they fooled many. But instead of radically changing their economies and installing a true democracy, they continued with the same Machiavellian procedure. They did not destroy the statues of their heroes; they instead kept them well maintained. The

197

new "property owners" would be the same administrators of their businesses; and if they were in those positions, it is because they were good comrades. But the majority of their businesses were not privatized. Capitalism was mainly just what Western investors did. It would be the West's own businesses that made jobs and even provided a qualified labor force. They would work with what was possible with the money that they loaned them, at the expense of jobs and on the dime of the citizens of the West. Later, when they believed it convenient, excuses to return to the totalitarian regime would abound. They predicted it all: the corruption would be the scapegoat for all the irregularities the ingenuous capitalists would see. A great part of what they invest in the West is invested in strategic enterprises by supposed businessmen and with the same funds that were loaned to them by the West. And from within, like the Trojan horse, they keep buying businesses of all types and funding the media. Also they gave support to many production studios for movies and television with which they leave a seed in peoples subconscious, the idea of official corruption, of vices of all types, or immorality, or disrespect for the law, disrespect for parents, for the authorities and for the values of one's country, and the values of one's religion, just as they sew doubt, fear, lack of faith and confidence in society, in the authorities and the free enterprise system. The objective: to confuse, demoralize, corrupt, make believe that all are corrupt, evil, drug addicts, killers, homosexuals, unclean and idiotic, that the system does not work, that everything is rotting, as if the only normal ones were the one's actually seeing the movies. Unfortunately many movies did not advertise that they were made precisely to corrupt those that see them. Now it is difficult to get a good movie. And this has been occurring for some time. Even in 1980 there existed some of these productions. It is not strange then that things have gotten worse because that was the purpose of these movies and the studios that produced them: to corrupt and humiliate North American society. And now there are even more "studios" that produce this genre of movies and reports, even within the United States itself, with this malevolent end.

They are the real creators of the evils and disgraces that we are living. They infiltrate even the churches as preachers. It is a cancer that grows day by day. Time is running out. And if things continue as they are going and the intelligent people on the left do not react, nor do the true democrats, and they permit these things to keep corrupting and demoralizing free countries, very soon the global power could be in their hands, and we would all be enslaved.

And what do they win by this? What would be the merit in destroying what everyone knows is good, in order to impose a failed system that the whole world detests for its falsehood and inhumanity? What is the merit in making people believe that something that they believe is completely bad is actually good, and that what doesn't help them has been proved to be good? Is it not preferable to perfect what has been proven to work, before destroying it to impose something that has nothing that works?

And if they persist in doing away with the free enterprise system, there are many calamities and scarcities that would present themselves. We are already seeing scarcity in some foods at a worldwide level; as we all know, in all the countries where the enemies of private property take power, the production of foods and other important goods decreases enormously. They will probably have to take drastic measures and lose some liberties and luxuries to conserve others. And this is already occurring; there are already many inconveniences that we are going through in airports and customs because of the enemies of private property that traffic drugs and train or arm terrorists.

WHY STILL THESE OLD AND FAILED THEORIES?

Concepts like equality, distribution of wealth, surplus value, exploitation of men by men, or considering religion the opiate of the masses, are all flawed or very badly analyzed.

Today we know very well that leftist totalitarian regimes have the largest inequality and the largest degree of exploitation of men by men. That people have no other alternative than submitting themselves to the sole owner or all-powerful party that imposes all the rules that they must obey. And with respect to religions, mislabeled by Marx as "the opiate of the masses," they have been so invalidated by the left that now, just as they do with the media, they use them for manipulating believers so that they permit or help the left to take global power. How do they do it? For example, if the government of the country where they operate is not leftist, they can induce people to protest in order to discredit and destabilize the government. But if the government is leftist and unbearable like the current government of Venezuela, they can keep believers like little sheep, telling them that all that is occurring is the will of God.

But how can they seek to eliminate an economic and political system that has proved itself to be capable of satisfying the material and spiritual needs of all, in order to impose another obsolete and failed system and has never been able to progress if it is not precisely with the help of the system they want to replace? How can they want to eliminate a very efficient system and its free citizens, in order to impose another inefficient one full of slaves? Can they want to eliminate a system that has the extraordinary merit of progressing despite the enormous damage of the perennial aggression of the leftists?

200

What future could we have with a system whose only methods of putting it in practice are either through trickery or force? Will they know that we lose not only everything that is good that we know the free enterprise system has, but also what in addition we could have achieved without the severe and intentional damages, or better yet working and collaborating to make it better? And how many other things would we lose that because of our customs we do not see nor value today? Will they be conscious that they eliminate those who feed them, that they destroy the system that provides for them, under which they live and enjoy life pleasantly? Perhaps they will be like the parasitic plant that attaches itself to a healthy plant in order to feed itself and in return weakens the host plant until it is killed? But the plant does not think, it does not realize that it is eliminating that on which it feeds, that when the host dies it will die as well.

We know that currently there are many problems in countries with free enterprise systems. But, perhaps the majority of these problems are caused precisely by the enemies of private property. How would this society be if those who work so furiously to destroy it, instead worked to perfect it?

And if the enemies of free enterprise succeed in disarming the United States and take global power, would we not automatically lose independence and liberty? And under whose orders would we be? Will they take into account our ideas, our way of life, our customs, and our worries? What type of treatment will they give up? Could we return to our former system of government? Who could we turn to after all the countries are subjugated? Who could we go to when we begin to find ourselves hungry and without our necessities, as we surely will? Will the party functionaries stop eating so that their people will have something to eat? What countries would be able to help us when every country will need help? What could be gained then by blaming the capitalists? Would it not be more intelligent to keep the hen that lays golden eggs instead of wishing her sick or killing her?

201

The paradox is that the enemies of private property in their native countries, party and commemorate independence and pride themselves on their liberators, and yet the truth is that they want to take us blindfolded to a place where we depend on foreign powers, with different customs and even different ways of speaking. Powers that did not doubt in using the most criminal means to keep their own countrymen subjugated. And if we know of the unmerciful treatment that they received, what can foreigners hope for, least of all the Latinos? Could we gain back our independence and liberty? Unfortunately, democracies still lack adequate self-defense, which any natural organism has in order to defend itself from its natural enemies, and which our own body has to defend itself from microbes and viruses.

And if, even knowing the true causes of the state of our people, and as other countries developed a free enterprise system in such a short time, what role will the caring leftist play who really wants the best for everyone? Will they have the sufficient determination and bravery to turn everything upside down and work for the side of justice, democracy, and liberty?

If these leftist regimes really worked, why then should we hope that the system that "does not work" will bring well-being and prosperity? Why are they not capable of prospering without the help of the ingenuous capitalists and without robbing money from them? Why do they not first prove that they can prosper in freedom, democracy, and without help of free nations? What satisfaction can they feel upon trying to make believe that the society in which everyone wants to live "does not work", or in trying to make believe that the society in which nobody wants to live "does work?" It would seem that it is not the well being of the people that they want but instead to get power for power's sake, with no concern for the fact they are tricking or manipulating everyone. On the contrary, they could not look to discredit and destroy this society, to which they owe almost everything, including the fact that they are able to eat. Because if a regular system of government was so good, why would they need force or trickery to impose it? What would they need the help of the ingenuous capitalists? How can they seek to eliminate a system that in addition to providing them with a sufficient supply of food and giving them a large variety of luxuries and services, also contributes with food, resources, technology, along with its people in order to help the ungrateful leftists get out of their state of insufficiency and backwardness?

Now they want to monopolize information and opinion in order to take everyone over the same cliff. They want to impede all discernment that can help them see the error that they are taking part in. They want to silence those who do not want to live in a regime of this type. They want to hide all the crimes, failures, and injustices that they have committed along the way. What could we hope for from those who take power based on lies, omitting the greatest truths, permitting all that is bad, and destroying all spiritual and material moral values?

It is probable that those that direct the left from the top, educated in the philosophy of using any means to arrive at any end, will never stop using them, and will continue tricking themselves. And it follows: How could there be confidence amongst them? How could they know who lies and who tells the truth?

Let us suppose that the whole world is now in the hands of the left. Naturally, every leader will have his own ideas and aspirations and will think that he is completely right. And as good leftists, will they perhaps stop justifying any means to achieve their ends? How could they even believe what another leftist is saying? How could they know who lies and who tells the truth, what with all the secret pacts that they have made amongst themselves? When and where were such pacts respected by the leftists?

Do you imagine living in a world in which everyone has to accept (true or not) what the masters instill in us as good, or as bad, or as just or unjust? Perhaps the high-up leftist leaders do not know at these heights how to construct a country? Perhaps we do not see how they bring in private investors to all countries where the people want progress? And if they already know how to bring well being to their countries, why then do they not admit it? Why do they continue damaging those who help them? Why do they continue to bend or subjugating everyone?

My leftist friends, you more than anyone can avoid total subjugation. Do not forget that it is certain that they are using you so that they can throw you out with the garbage later. Perhaps the end does not justify all the means? No one knows the good things he has until he loses them. And in that case, it would be too late because that loss is irreversible.

We are then very close to losing our most valuable possession, that of being able to do with our lives what we please. And the pretext is the common good. For the common good they would do us the worst common wrongdoing: we would be enslaved. And we might possibly not even be conscious of it, because not one would tell us. Because we would be enslaved in mind and body, the worst type of slavery. They would tell us everything. The word slave would be used exclusively to refer to the time when masters sold slaves and beat them with whips. We would no long act according to our criteria, but instead in the way that the master wanted. We would be domesticated like the dog, horse, or camel. And though the most authentic Marxists do not believe in God or in religions, it is possible that they would make a single religion, which they would modify and accommodate at their convenience. What is good, beautiful or valuable would not be what any one man thinks, but rather what they indoctrinate us with. And it is happening. If the painter is a leftist, no matter how he paints he is a good painter. If the singer is a leftist, no matter how she sings, she is a great singer. If the movie was made to corrupt and demoralize capitalist society and devalue the free enterprise system, it is a great movie and they give it important awards. If the writer is a leftist, however he writes, he is a great writer. The masters will be the only ones with the right to think, everyone else will worship them. And those who share their ideas will with difficulty take it into account. It is disheartening to see how a regime of our time could impose itself by using trickery, fear, crime, kidnapping, drug trafficking, multi-million dollar robberies, terror, evil, and all of the bad things that exist in the world. And the most unfortunate, that there are people collaborating with them. Some because they still believe in these failed theories. Others because they are fearful. Others because they prefer that the party take care of them, because maybe they do not feel capable of making a living any other way. And others because they do not support the idea of some people living a little better than others and they prefer to see everyone living in poverty, although poverty never comes to the masters.

THE NEW DICTATORSHIPS

They are leftists; they possess and control the majority, or all of the media, and because of this they tend to perpetuate and multiply in an accelerated manner at a world level. And they differentiate themselves from other dictatorships because they simulate democracy by permitting certain opposition in scarce media outlets, also from the left, that many think are part of the Right.

The best example: the current regime in Venezuela, where the very leftists themselves are those who make the opposition. And although they do not like Chavez, they prefer to continue with him rather than risking losing along with the Right in impartial elections. And this has meant the destruction of a great part of the country, and thousands of dead people, ruined, unemployed, exiled, imprisoned, kidnapped, assassinated, emigrated or separated from their families.

Unfortunately, when we were giving thanks to God, believing that this was the end of the dictatorship, and we were electing a provisional government presided over by Carmona Estanga in 2002, a government that tried to dissolve other powers that the dictator had had, the leftist media fell upon her, including the international channel CNN, calling the new government a coup and they brought the dictator back. And in what other way does one leave a dictatorship behind? Perhaps it is possible to take out only the dictator and leave the other powers intact, including the electoral powers? Who would have won in the next elections? Because of this, the big problem currently in Venezuela is not so much Chavez, but rather the media that is in the hands of the Left. Because of this, they preferred to bring back the dictator, rather than lose the other powers that were also in the hands of the left. For this reason they did not interview people from the Right. Because of this, in all these years none of these media outlets has interviewed ex-presidents, nor military exiles abroad, not even to ask them what

206

happened to Carmona Estanga, the supposed coup leader. And because of this, they continue talking about democracy and they continue calling the dictator president.

And it is not that a real and large opposition does not exist in Venezuela. If in any country there are democrats and supporters of private property with leadership qualities, it is in Venezuela. Many are in foreign exile, among which are military leaders and ex-presidents. Others are in prison. And the great majority is in the street. But they cannot be known because the media does not interview them, nor does it support them, nor does it publish their writings or opinions. However, there are still good and important democrats in the opposition that has been almost completely ignored by the media. They only interview them when serious differences exist between the leftists. But there is no doubt that the large majority of Venezuelans are against the dictatorship, although their hands are tied, in such a way that they can't even verify the facts from the National Electoral Council.

A good example of how the media operates, even those media outlets that claim to be oppositional, we could observe at the beginning of 2009 with the surprising and intense media campaign to hold a referendum to reelect Chavez "indefinitely." From this occurrence (applying the wise Biblical phrase: "By their fruits you will know them.") we perceive the left's plan is to field Chavez as a candidate, as many times as necessary, until they get the main parties to accept a sole candidate that may be equally leftist, in order to then change the president. It is for this reason that Venezuelans will only see Chavez leave power when they present another leftist candidate to face him. In other words, when the leftist dictatorship can accommodate another leftist in the presidency. This is the answer to so many questions that we, the Venezuelans, asked ourselves: Why does the media, including Globovision and Radio Caracas TV (supposedly oppositional), continue playing the game in this way? That instead of ignoring it, or criticizing it harshly, did they try to convince us that we were to go out again to vote?

207

Why did this same media make all Venezuelans violate the Constitution? Why were they making us vote again for what we had already rejected? Why did they make us waste time, patience, and the money of the Venezuelan people? Why did they not instead criticize the National Election Commission and the other powers for permitting this violation? Why make our lives more bitter? Why did the media, including Globovision and Radio Caracas TV insist on going through with the proposal? Why then, instead of interviewing the obliging people that recommended that we go in to vote, knowing that it was impossible to win with the electoral power in the hands of the dictatorship, did they not interview all of the distinguished Venezuelans who deplored this new and flagrant joke and at the same time violation of the constitution that they themselves wrote? Why did they not wage a campaign to destroy it and put it to justice for such serious crimes? Or why did they not interview candidates for governor and mayor that complained of fraud in recently celebrated elections? Or why did they not wage a campaign so that the main parties had representation in the Nation Electoral Council? Or why not ignore the dictator instead of ignoring for so many years the ex-presidents and all of the other political exiles? Perhaps they were obligated to comply with the regime? And if that were so, why did they not say it, or interview people that would say it, instead of tricking the people by keeping an appearance of democracy, and making all of us Venezuelans lose time and patience.

Now let us imagine the media that supposedly is with the opposition, ignoring the dictator. Let them never mention him again. That after the *Hello President* or the abusive radio and television broadcasts, they did not make commentaries, and on making them, they were only to criticize the despotic abuse of confiscating all radio and television channels in the country as many times as they wanted and any time that they wanted. And what would happen when the media did not now even mention the dictator? Would he not lose the little popularity that he still held on to?

There are so few Venezuelans that view these abusive channels, that they could even pass undetected, if it weren't for the media that supposedly are in the opposition, that charge themselves with making us know about all of them, what the dictator said, and how he said it and why he said it. They even go so far as to repeat it every second for the entire world to be able to realize it.

Without a doubt: it is the media that gives importance to the dictator. It is the media that makes propaganda. It is the media that keep him in power.

And why do they do this? Because lamentably those media outlets that supposedly are in the opposition, are also in the hands of the left. And why do they want to present Chavez as a candidate? Because without him, all the political parties could present candidates for the presidency without any problem, and it is very probable that one from the right would win. On the other hand, with the threat of Chavez as a candidate, there would always be the pretext of looking for a different candidate to go against him, and then the Left would not stop until they had made sure that that candidate was also leftist. If they do not find such a candidate, as they manipulate the political lens of the nation, they would latch onto Chavez again even knowing how sickened the people are by him and the tragedy that it is for Venezuela and for all Venezuelans.

It is for this reason that all the media in the hands of the left, instead of ignoring Chavez, repeat every second his vulgar and boastful gossip, in order to keep him in the public eye. And it is also for this reason that the candidates selected to go against the regime are chosen in secret, or through arbitration of electoral power, so that the people do not realize the stubbornness of the left in refusing to let go of petroleum. None of this could occur if the Venezuelans could count on an electoral power represented by and watched over by all political organizations and with a truly democratic constitution, and contemplated the second round as much for presidential elections as for gubernatorial and mayoral elections. So all candidates could compete, from which only the two most popular from the primary would go to a general election so that no governors are elected by just a few, instead by more than half the voters. However, despite its importance, not even the media that is supposedly oppositional has worried about correcting this serious flaw, and they prefer the difficult task of agreeing on a different candidate, who is of course from the left. For this reason they waged a surprising and intense campaign to bring up Chavez newly and indefinitely as a candidate without caring that they were violating the Constitution again. It is also for this reason that in all these years they did not denounce this dictatorship, and they continue calling the dictator president. And is it also because of this that the people are brought to elections as is they were really part of a democracy.

These dictatorships begin forming with the seizure of the media, figureheads of the left, the same left of which they claim to be owners. And with the media taken, they can bring to the presidency even the most inappropriate of candidates. And so that the people vote for him they interview him every second in order to keep him in the spotlight; they ask him stupid questions so he can look good; they let him talk as much as he wants and they publish anything he says.

Later, with the savage now as president, they begin seizing the other powers, by violating norms, laws, and rules, while the media ignores the irregularities and violations.

Of course, the first thing they do is take the Electoral Power, never again to give it up. This is the key to not losing another election. And now you can imagine whom they will invite to the next elections as international observers.

Meanwhile, in the armed forces in addition to changing the Minister of Defense, they dismiss good and competent officers from key command posts and bring leftists into those positions without considering how inept they may be. And on taking the armed forces, there is now no way of ending the dictatorship, as long as the leftists want it to remain.

THE MIRROR OF A TYRANT IN VENEZUELA

Let's look at ourselves in the mirror. Fortunately, it is a local situation. But it helps us visualizes a similar drama on the world stage.

And we say similar because happily we are in front of the whole world, and because of this the same leftists people could still partially control it and denounce it. But in the global stage things would be very different.

Let's imagine ourselves for a moment that other countries didn't exist, that the world was only Venezuela. Do you think that Chavez would voluntarily give up power? Or perhaps he would have stopped all these damaging and criminal occurrences? And what would have happened to those who did not support him, or those who criticized him, or with those who do not agree with his methods of government? Perhaps they would have dared to tell him anything to the contrary? Would the most valiant or daring not be dead or imprisoned? And the rest, what would they have been able to do? It would be exactly the same on a global stage. Let us not forget that they would equally control all the powers. They would control the whole armed forces and all media and opinion outlets, which equally would be purged of all who dissent or oppose. Let us remember that this has to do with maintaining power. Or would they perhaps stop doing what is "convenient" to their appetites? Or perhaps the ends would not continue justifying all the means? The same would have happened with Chavez if the world circumscribed itself upon Venezuela, power would become monopolized and globalized.

Will it have crossed the mind of the well-intentioned, leftist Venezuelans and those from other countries that have been used for a while now, and later will be throw into the garbage can? Will the same Chavez be conscious that they are using him in order to later eliminate him and throw him out with the garbage, him more than anyone else? Remember

212

that all is fair in order to get and maintain power. And is there perhaps something strange about the fact that for a long time now they have been giving out high doses of the same medicine? Perhaps they ignore the fact that they are traveling on the same road of servitude and submission? Where there will exist only two classes: the one that give orders and the one that must obey, the masters and the slaves. And who would dare to contradict their master? Do they think that they can oppose him?

On the other hand, who is going to believe that now the ringleaders of the international left do not know how to bring comfort and well-bing to all citizens of the world, even in complete liberty? Who is going to believe that they don't know the secrets to transform and develop whichever country? Is it not precisely for this reason that capitalists exist in all parts of the world in order to create wealth in the countries that are still subjugated? Perhaps someone thinks that the directors of the Left do not know how to eradicate war, violence, and crime? Or perhaps they think that they ignore what is good and what is bad for them in the free enterprise system. How different would things be if all this effort that they have put in in order to damage the countries with a free enterprise system, made them better in order to perfect them and bring more well being to the neediest! How different the world would be! How many lost years! What a loss of will and work! How many senseless deaths! How much misery and sterile destruction!

Could it be that the well-intentioned leftists do not see what is at the end of the tunnel; that by monopolizing information and opinion and all the economic and political power, they are creating a gigantic monopoly with only one director whom all will be obliged to obey? Perhaps they do not see that they drive us into a trap from which it will be difficult to escape? Could it be that they do not see how difficult it would be to return to being independent, and that nothing would help them be forgiven? It's a shame to see how for a foreign and enslaving cause they spend so many

213

financial and human resources! With what force would developing countries be able to earn respect, even if they had the best technology?

Only in certain countries and for a very short time has democracy been able to be maintained. The history of man has been a constant struggle to monopolize all power. History has been a series of dictatorial empires in which someone becomes a god, whom all fear and should obey. Without going too far, there are still witnesses, and despite great opposition by the whole world, one of these- Hitler-almost exterminated the Jews. And another in Russia –Stalin-killed more than 20 million of his countrymen. If they did this despite worldwide protest, what would they be capable of doing when there is no opposition? Remember that there are no morals, no ethics, no principles, and no people that matter. And as today all ways to gain power are acceptable, in the same way they would justify themselves to maintain power. They would never permit any type of opposition. And what would be the next action steps to take? Perhaps they will come to think that their actions are wrong? Who would dare to contradict them? What heads of state –surely unarmed and given their position by the leftists themselves- would dare to confront them? Lamentably, we are at the edge of an abyss. Because of this, my friends, I invite you to reflect, in a special way, because you all are those who still can do something in order to change the path we are on.

A GREAT INEQUALITY

While we observe the United States being economically mistreated, and its sphere of political and military influence reduced, on the other hand we witness the dangerous economic and political expansionism of countries like Russia and China with totalitarian leftist regimes, the most closed and repressive in the world. The cynical aspect of this is that these countries prosper thanks to multimillion-dollar loans, technical help, multimillion-dollar investments, and preferential treatment in commerce that is offered to them by this benevolent and mistreated country (the USA). Observing this great inequality causes us to reflect on the great risks that humanity runs if countries and organizations like the UN and OAS (which owe their existence to the United States) continue this unjust treatment of the United States.

We understand by the term neutrality, the political and economic posture adopted by those countries who want to maintain a just and balanced relationship with antagonistic and distinct powers on which they depend in one way or another, and that, in order to be able to defend themselves from one, they make the support of the other indispensible. It is a categorical truth: one may only be neutral and independent while different powers exist that can balance one another, and only while one is either in good standing with all of them, or without an alliance with either of them. Naturally this would be the most comfortable and advantageous position for whichever country, as much militarily in order to not become mixed up in foreign conflicts, as economically in order to try to benefit from both parties. The great problem is that this balance is easily lost, and that governments of countries considered supposedly independent today, because of their orientation in foreign relations, as much political as economic. And upon losing this equilibrium, a progressive weakening would follow, pushing for the building up of the other side that will end in

215

the annihilation of one over the other. When this occurs, neutrality and independence are irreparably done with, and all countries will become territories on a single empire.

All of our heroes of independence: Washington, Bolivar, Marti, Santander, fought to make us politically free and independent. And if our governors wanted our countries to continue being free and independent they would have then watched over us and acted in order to maintain this balance. However, as this is very difficult, the best thing to do is to move away from neutrality and to put ourselves on the side of that country that we are most confident in, where human rights are most respected, where people are happier with the system of government, and in which they sympathize with and to which they adapt better. This government is certainly in a free country and democratic country. To continue being neutral would equate to permitting the dominion of the most tyrannical and enslaving power, with untold consequences.

DISARMAMENT

Is a total nuclear disarmament beneficial? Could this save the world from an atomic war? What is the probability of that type of war?

We could consider disarmament the greatest defeat of free nations. Upon disarming the United States they can now subjugate us sooner and without risk. Also, countries in the hands of the left never follow through on disarmament pacts. Such pacts only serve to disarm the United States

Many could plan a third world war with all imaginable military power and diabolical armaments. But it would be very difficult for this to occur. And the reason is from a convincing logic: the instinct of self-preservation, no one likes to die or kill their own people, and even less in this way.

It is very easy to prepare other countries for their own suicide so that they fall to pieces. But it is a much different thing to prepare oneself to destroy oneself in addition to one's own country and family. Speaking clearly, no one in his or her right mind would think to initiate a nuclear war because it would be a collective suicide. However, there will always be the possibility that one of the powers, sensing itself roped in would prefer to do away with everyone, before seeing itself humiliated and defeated. And this is the risk that we attempt to eliminate with nuclear disarmament. But it could also be the most important defeat that free countries suffer in this unjust and camouflaged war that is fought today. We can see who would win the third war and who would lose upon reading newspapers, listening to the radio, or watching television. There we find out about the governments that fall and those that begin each day, if they are from the left or from the right. We find out about the electoral processes in "democratic" countries: who will govern, with what ideas, and what side they favor, if they

217

collaborate with free countries or with leftist totalitarianism. We can also realize how the United Nations or the Organization of American States are biased, just like the media, from how they place the news, from how them emphasize some stories, while omitting or hiding others. We also can observe how they are preparing future professionals in our "democratic" universities, if they are teaching the good about free enterprise and the failure of Marxism, or if it is the opposite. We can also observe editorial shows, and the biases of the "analysts" that are interviewed, if they are in favor of the left or if they are with the right, if in free enterprising countries they are building culture or if they are corrupting and demoralizing the people. And if we are good observers, we will realize that the left is overwhelmingly winning this war, because they control the majority of the media and opinion outlets. And it is because of this that every time there are more governing politicians from the left and fewer from the right, that leftists dictators are welcomed even in free and democratic countries, and conversely those of the right, if they even remain, are not even wanted in their same "democratic" countries. But the greatest advantage that countries with leftist regimes have is that these regimes permit no internal opposition; all of the media and opinion outlets are in their hands. All this occurs while in these free enterprising, democratic countries leftists take advantage of the kindnesses and liberties of this system in order to buy or install new media and opinion outlets.

On the other hand, proportionally to its inhabitants, the countries controlled by the left have the biggest militaries, in contrast with many free countries that don't even have an army. Said in another way, the left does not need nuclear force in order to conquer the planet. If it succeeds in disarming the United States, it will have won the Third World War. On the other hand, the United States, which might need its nuclear force, (to dissuade) being then still completely isolated and without the help of other countries, would always be respected while they peel away their nuclear teeth. Unfortunately, we can only be free and independent while the United States remains free and independent. If they fall, we will also fall. Consequently, the best policy that the United States adopts for its defense and against the hoarding of global power will also be the best policy for all who want to always live freely and independently. It will also be the best for all who do no want to live perpetually subjugated.

SUBMISSION

If things continue as they are now, world power could be in the hands of the totalitarian left very soon. Because we all know that its goal is to dominate the world, and to this end they strengthen themselves politically and economically, thanks in part to naivety and the good faith of North America and other democrats of the free world that help them with great investments and technology. And partly because of the weakness of democratic countries that permit, like the Trojan Horse, being undermined from within, and for which they use the means of information and opinion, as in movies and reports, in order to corrupt North American society. In effect, we see a thousand movies or reports and in all of them we see evil, corruption, perverseness, filth, and sexual depravity. They want to make us believe that in the United States everyone violates the law, and that every couple is unfaithful, that everyone is abnormal, and that it is a place filled with only idiots, thieves, criminals, drug addicts, the unclean, lesbians, and homosexuals. And they are achieving this goal. They are corrupting us. They add to this in the same United States and in the other countries of the free world, the blindness or ingenuousness of journalists, politicians, and intellectuals, as some sort of Trojan horse, who make idiots useful when they propose one-way pacifism, meaning that those totalitarian leftist countries can attack their neighbors and they do not protest. And these continual protests, many times make the United States revoke its support of the attacked, in order to allow them to be taken by the Marxists and to incline the balance more in favor of leftist totalitarianism. And to follow that tendency (unless there is a nuclear conflict, which is less than likely) would end in the annihilation of democracy and liberty. And we believe that the only way of avoiding it is to leave indifference behind and take the side of those who respect human rights, are more trustworthy and where the people are happiest with their system of government. That place is without a doubt the United States of America.

And for what other reasons should we be with the North Americans? Because despite the nickname of imperialist that the leftist propaganda pegs them with, they have never been territorially expansionist. They did not do it in the Second World War when they were the only ones that possessed the atomic bomb, and where they perfectly well could have dominated the world, and could even have gotten rid of Communism. Nor did they annex territories, or even charge them the costs of the war. And while Russia made firewood from the fallen tree, and imposed its system and its domination on many European countries, the United States implemented the Marshall Plan in order to help all the war-ravaged countries, including its rivals. They also founded the United Nations and the Organization of American States with the primordial end of preserving peace, and collecting funds to help the neediest countries. Unfortunately, the left also took possession of these international organizations, which are still today completely partial to leftist governments.

Certainly, since the Second World War, the United States has been on the defensive. However, for the same pressures from the left, and from the "pacifists" and environmentalists that only protest in capitalist countries, they could not avoid the fall of many countries under the yoke of totalitarian leftists. And it does not seem strange that very soon world power could be in the hands of leftist totalitarians. And then, perhaps we could impede them subjecting us to such occurrences? Could a regional leader perhaps from those that today collaborate to globalize that power stop them? And what would be some of its immediate actions? Let's reflect: if the Germans, intelligent and civilized, were under a dictatorship that was capable of doing away with almost all Jews, and the Communists were capable of killing more than 20 million compatriots, and of having the world against them, what would they be capable of doing if they come to dominate the world when they have no opposition? Is it true that the means by which they reach their ends have been important to them? And what will happen to the Latinos? Are we so ingenuous as to think that they will

221

share the power with us? How will they treat us? Will they have consideration for us? And to whom could we go in search of help, be it to eat, or to protect us from their abuses? Who will guarantee the least respect for human rights? Do they have morals and scruples? Is it that they have tried the contrary? If they are capable of killing their own comrades that have given them their best years and still, it is enough that they think a little differently, that they cease to be robots, to justify getting rid of them without mercy. Example abound. If religion does not exist for them, if morals do not exist for them, if they are complete materialists, what would they be capable of doing when they have absolute power over the Earth? Will they perhaps stop doing what they see as "most convenient?" For example: will they decide to exterminate or castrate blacks because they simply have no sympathy for them? Or the indigenous? Or the Jews? Or the mulattos or mestizos for being "impure?" Or the mentally handicapped? Or the homosexuals? Or bald people? Or the ugly? Or the beautiful? Or those with big noses? Or whomever else they look upon? This is only one example of what could really occur, but even worse things could happen, things that are difficult for us to imagine today. I hope, then, that all who in one way or another collaborate so that this could soon be a reality, reflect and help the world bring about this reality to free and democratic nations. That they go down in history as defenders of liberty and not like Judas who gave them over to new masters. On the other hand, how could we get out of the poverty that they are leadings us to if they ruin the United States and the businesses that are still in good enough condition to invest? Perhaps our countries are not going to need investors in order to take us forward as they are doing now in China? How could we get ourselves out of misery and scarcity if they ruin those that could help us, be it with investment or consumption of our products? Why, then, instead of damaging them do we not take care of the health of these countries? We are either with God or the Devil. Not doing anything serious would let them take global power, and because of that it would be the same as letting ourselves become subjugated.

THE PARTY AND ITS DISAPPEARANCE

If the whole world came to be subject to the Marxists, at the beginning, with no other existing alternative, all people would logically want to be part of the Party. All would want to belong to it as something vitally important to obtain a better job, a better career, or even a good bureaucratic position. And when everyone belongs to the party, with time Party membership would stop becoming a requirement to get better treatment or a better job, because it would be common knowledge that everyone belonged to it. And at ceasing to be a requirement, naturally it would not be lacking. And if party membership were not lacking, it would cease to exist.

And after perhaps a number of years we would probably go back to the same condition we are in now. The most capable people, the most intelligent, the most worried and willful, would be without a doubt, those who would keep the most important positions. The important positions would be occupied by precisely the same people that overcome their circumstances in the free enterprise system. And probably these people would give more liberties and private property to the rest and free enterprise would return.

Meanwhile they would have lost perhaps a few centuries of progress and would not have the same way of imagining possibilities. Only by imagining, as today we can imagine the backward state of the world if we had imposed Communism on all, in those days when the Manifesto was published, or as today we can picture the degree of progress which we would have achieved if the Communists with all their intentional evils would have disappeared from that point on, and we would all have worked honestly for democracy, peace, progress and well-being of all peoples of the world.

FINAL MESSAGE

We hope for the reader, upon finishing this book, to have a much more clear vision of the relationship that exists between politics and economic effects that affect all of us. We want them to have knowledge of who created the majority of the evils that we suffer in this world, of why the free enterprise system is better, of why price regulation, labor immobility and salary increases by decree are detrimental. We hope that this book contributes to our exit from this distressing path that we are now on, and leads us to better governments and a better world. We want everyone, according to his possibilities, to contribute his grain of sand in order to evade total subjugation, so that they, he or she may help to establish true democracies, where the public officials are at the service of the citizenry and not the citizens at the service of the officials. And where all can live without the fear and humiliation that those who find themselves subjugated experience.

Adolfo García Mendez

INDEX